# The Art of Modern Gastronomy

Techniques and Recipes for the Contemporary Chef

## Queenie Cobb

The presentation of the information is without contract or any type of guarantee assurance. The trademarks that are used are without any consent, and the publication of the trademark is without permission or backing by the trademark owner. All trademarks and brands within this book are for clarifying purposes only and are the owned by the owners themselves, not affiliated with this document.

# Table of Contents

# Chapter 1

# Introduction to Modern Gastronomy

## The Evolution of Culinary Arts

Culinary arts have evolved in tandem with human civilization, reflecting changes in culture, technology, and societal norms. The journey of culinary arts begins with the rudimentary cooking methods of our ancestors and extends to the sophisticated techniques of contemporary cuisine. This evolution is not just a tale of technological advancements but also one of cultural exchange, creativity, and an ever-expanding understanding of food science.

In the earliest days, cooking was a necessity for survival. Early humans discovered that fire could transform raw ingredients into more palatable and digestible forms, marking the inception of cooking. Roasting over open flames was likely the first method, followed by boiling and steaming using rudimentary vessels. These initial techniques laid the groundwork for more complex culinary practices. As societies formed and agriculture developed, food preparation began to reflect the variety of available ingredients and the emerging cultural practices.

Ancient civilizations, such as the Egyptians, Greeks, and Romans, made significant contributions to culinary arts. The Egyptians are known for their use of spices and herbs to enhance flavor and preserve food. They cultivated a variety of plants and developed techniques for baking bread, a staple that persists in modern diets. The Greeks introduced the concept of gastronomy, emphasizing the pleasure of eating and the importance of balanced meals. They also developed early forms of culinary documentation, with recipes that detailed ingredients and methods. The Romans, with their vast empire, became masters of culinary synthesis, incorporating ingredients and techniques from the far reaches of their territory. They were known for elaborate feasts and the use of sauces to complement dishes, a precursor to modern gastronomy.

The Middle Ages saw the rise of elaborate banquet culture, particularly in Europe. The feudal system concentrated wealth and power among the nobility, who indulged in lavish feasts as a display of wealth and status. Spices imported from Asia became highly prized, and their use in cooking indicated affluence. This period also saw the development of early culinary guilds, which standardized practices and advanced the professional status of cooks. Monastic communities contributed to culinary evolution by preserving agricultural knowledge and culinary manuscripts, ensuring that techniques and recipes were passed down through generations.

The Renaissance marked a significant turning point in the culinary arts, paralleling advancements in science, exploration, and art. The discovery of the New World introduced European kitchens to a plethora of new ingredients, such as tomatoes, potatoes, and chocolate, which revolutionized cooking. This period also saw the publication of the first modern cookbooks, which disseminated knowledge and allowed culinary techniques to spread more widely. Chefs began to emerge as artists in their own right, experimenting with flavors and presentation to create dishes that were not only delicious but visually stunning.

The 17th and 18th centuries witnessed the refinement of French cuisine, which would come to dominate Western culinary arts. The establishment of professional kitchens in the courts of French nobility led to the development of haute cuisine, characterized by meticulous preparation, the use of high-quality ingredients, and elaborate presentation. The publication of François Pierre La Varenne's "Le Cuisinier François" and later, Marie-Antoine Carême's works, laid the foundations for classical French cuisine. Carême, in particular, is often hailed as the first celebrity chef, known for his grand culinary creations and the systematization of kitchen practices.

The Industrial Revolution brought about profound changes in the culinary arts, driven by technological advancements and urbanization. The invention of kitchen appliances such as the stove and refrigerator transformed food preparation, making it more efficient and accessible. Canning and pasteurization improved food preservation, expanding the availability of ingredients regardless of season. The rise of the restaurant industry provided opportunities for chefs to showcase their talents to a broader audience, leading to increased professionalization and specialization within the culinary field.

The 20th century saw the emergence of various culinary movements, each contributing to the evolution of the art. The early part of the century was dominated by classical French cuisine, but post-World War II, there was a shift towards simplicity and the use of fresh, local ingredients. This movement, known as nouvelle cuisine, was spearheaded by chefs like Paul Bocuse and the Troisgros brothers. They rejected the heavy sauces and ornate presentations of classical cuisine in favor of lighter, more natural dishes.

Simultaneously, there was a growing interest in international cuisines, driven by increased travel and immigration. This period saw the introduction and popularization of Asian, African, and Latin American cuisines in Western countries, enriching the culinary landscape with diverse flavors and techniques. Fusion cuisine emerged as a new trend, blending elements from different culinary traditions to create innovative dishes.

The latter part of the 20th century and the early 21st century have been marked by a focus on sustainability and health. With growing awareness of environmental issues and the impact of food production on the planet, chefs and consumers alike have embraced farm-to-table practices, organic ingredients, and sustainable sourcing. This movement emphasizes the importance of supporting local producers and reducing food waste, aligning culinary practices with ecological responsibility.

Modern culinary arts are also deeply influenced by advancements in food science and technology. Molecular gastronomy, pioneered by chefs like Ferran Adrià and Heston Blumenthal, explores the physical and chemical transformations of ingredients during cooking. This scientific approach has led to innovative techniques such as spherification, foaming, and sous-vide cooking, which have expanded the boundaries of what is possible in the kitchen. These techniques allow chefs to create unique textures and flavors, transforming dining into a multi-sensory experience.

Another significant development in contemporary culinary arts is the rise of digital technology and social media. Platforms like Instagram and YouTube have transformed the way food is shared and consumed visually. Chefs and food enthusiasts can now reach a global audience, showcasing their creations and inspiring others. This democratization of culinary knowledge has led to a surge in home cooking and experimentation, with amateur cooks gaining access to professional-level techniques and recipes.

## Defining Modern Gastronomy

Modern gastronomy represents a confluence of tradition, innovation, and science, creating a culinary philosophy that transcends simple sustenance. It is a celebration of creativity, technology, and the endless pursuit of perfection in the kitchen. At its core, modern gastronomy seeks to elevate dining experiences, transforming meals into multisensory events that engage not just the palate, but also the eyes, nose, and even ears. Understanding this dynamic field requires a deep dive into its principles, practices, and the mindset that drives contemporary chefs.

One of the hallmarks of modern gastronomy is the emphasis on high-quality, often locally sourced ingredients. The farm-to-table movement epitomizes this focus, advocating for the use of fresh, seasonal produce that not only supports local farmers but also ensures peak flavor and nutritional value. Chefs today are deeply invested in knowing the origins of their ingredients, often visiting farms, fisheries, and markets to personally select the best available products. This hands-on approach fosters a deeper connection to the food and a greater appreciation for its journey from field to plate.

Innovative cooking techniques are another cornerstone of modern gastronomy. Sous vide, a method of cooking food in vacuum-sealed bags at precise, low temperatures, allows chefs to achieve perfect textures and flavors that are difficult to reproduce with traditional methods. Similarly, techniques borrowed from molecular gastronomy, such as spherification and foaming, enable chefs to manipulate the physical properties of ingredients, creating unexpected and delightful culinary experiences. These methods are not just about novelty; they are tools that chefs use to enhance and perfect their dishes, pushing the boundaries of what is possible in the kitchen.

The integration of science into cooking is a defining feature of modern gastronomy. Chefs collaborate with food scientists to understand the molecular interactions that occur during cooking, leading to better control over texture, flavor, and presentation. This scientific approach demystifies many aspects of cooking, providing chefs with the knowledge to replicate or innovate techniques with precision. The result is a more consistent and elevated culinary experience for diners.

Presentation and plating are given as much importance as the taste and texture of the food. Modern gastronomy views the plate as a canvas, and the food as an art form. Chefs employ techniques from visual arts to create dishes that are visually stunning, using color, texture, and composition to enhance the dining experience. Micro herbs, edible flowers, and intricately designed sauces are used not just for their flavors, but for their aesthetic contributions. This attention to detail transforms each dish into a piece of edible art, engaging diners' senses before they even take their first bite.

Sustainability and ethical considerations have become integral to modern gastronomy. Chefs are increasingly mindful of the environmental and social impacts of their ingredient choices, striving to reduce waste, support sustainable fishing practices, and minimize their carbon footprint. This commitment extends to the entire supply chain, from sourcing ingredients to energy-efficient kitchen practices. By prioritizing sustainability, modern gastronomy aims to create a positive impact on the planet while delivering exceptional dining experiences.

Cultural diversity and fusion cuisine are celebrated in modern gastronomy. Chefs draw inspiration from a global pantry, blending flavors and techniques from different culinary traditions to create unique and innovative dishes. This cross-cultural exchange enriches the culinary landscape, introducing diners to new flavors and combinations that they might not have encountered otherwise. The fusion of different cuisines also reflects the interconnectedness of the modern world, where boundaries are increasingly blurred, and culinary traditions are shared and reinterpreted.

The role of technology cannot be overstated in the realm of modern gastronomy. Advanced kitchen equipment, such as combi ovens, thermal immersion circulators, and high-powered blenders, enable chefs to execute precise and complex cooking techniques with ease. Digital tools and software aid in recipe development, menu planning, and inventory management, streamlining operations and allowing chefs to focus more on creativity and execution. Furthermore, social media and digital platforms have revolutionized how chefs share their work and engage with their audience, turning cooking into a more interactive and communal experience.

The dining experience itself has evolved, moving beyond traditional restaurant settings. Pop-up dinners, chef's tables, and interactive dining experiences challenge the conventional boundaries of eating out. Chefs are experimenting with different formats to create memorable and immersive experiences for their guests. These innovative dining formats often blur the lines between the kitchen and the dining room, allowing diners to witness the culinary process firsthand and engage more deeply with the food and the chef's vision.

Innovation in beverage pairing has also become a focal point in modern gastronomy. Sommeliers and mixologists work closely with chefs to create pairings that complement and enhance the flavors of the dishes. This collaboration extends beyond traditional wine pairings to include craft beers, artisanal cocktails, and non-alcoholic beverages. The goal is to create a harmonious and holistic dining experience where each element – food, drink, and ambiance – is thoughtfully curated to delight the senses.

Modern gastronomy also places a strong emphasis on education and mentorship. Chefs are often seen as educators, sharing their knowledge and passion with the next generation of culinary professionals. Culinary schools and training programs have adapted to include courses on modern techniques, sustainability, and food science, ensuring that new chefs are well-equipped to navigate the contemporary culinary landscape. This culture of continuous learning and innovation keeps the culinary arts dynamic and ever-evolving.

Personalization is another trend shaping modern gastronomy. Chefs are increasingly attentive to dietary preferences and restrictions, crafting menus that cater to a wide range of needs, from vegan and gluten-free options to allergen-free dishes. This level of customization ensures that every diner can enjoy a tailored and inclusive culinary experience. The ability to accommodate diverse dietary requirements not only broadens the appeal of modern gastronomy but also reflects a deeper understanding of and respect for individual preferences and health considerations.

The philosophy of modern gastronomy is deeply rooted in the pursuit of excellence and the joy of discovery. Chefs approach their craft with a sense of curiosity and a willingness to experiment, constantly seeking new ways to surprise and delight their guests. This spirit of innovation is what drives the continual evolution of culinary arts, pushing boundaries and redefining what is possible in the kitchen.

# Essential Equipment and Tools

A well-equipped kitchen is the backbone of any culinary endeavor, providing the necessary tools to turn raw ingredients into culinary masterpieces. For beginners, understanding which equipment and tools are essential can be overwhelming, but mastering this knowledge is crucial for efficiency and success in the kitchen. This chapter delves into the must-have items that form the foundation of a functional kitchen, offering practical advice on their selection, use, and maintenance.

At the heart of every kitchen lies a good set of knives. Investing in high-quality knives is paramount, as they are the workhorses of food preparation. A chef's knife, typically 8 to 10 inches long, is the most versatile and indispensable tool, suitable for chopping, slicing, and dicing a variety of ingredients. Complementing this are a paring knife for intricate tasks like peeling and trimming, and a serrated knife for cutting through bread and tomatoes. When selecting knives, balance and comfort are critical, so it's wise to handle different brands and models before making a purchase. Regular sharpening and proper storage in a knife block or magnetic strip will ensure longevity and performance.

Cookware is another essential category, and the right pots and pans can significantly impact cooking results. A good starter set includes a non-stick skillet, a stainless steel sauté pan, a Dutch oven, and a saucepan. Non-stick skillets are perfect for eggs and delicate fish, while stainless steel pans withstand high heat and are ideal for browning meats and making pan sauces. Dutch ovens, with their heavy, thick walls, are perfect for slow-cooking stews and braises. Saucepans are versatile for making sauces, boiling pasta, and reheating leftovers. When choosing cookware, consider materials that provide even heat distribution, such as stainless steel with an aluminum or copper core.

Baking enthusiasts will find a few key items indispensable. A set of mixing bowls, preferably in stainless steel or glass, is essential for combining ingredients. Measuring cups and spoons ensure precision, which is particularly important in baking. A sturdy rolling pin, baking sheets, and a variety of baking pans – including a loaf pan, muffin tin, and cake pans – round out the basics. Silicone baking mats or parchment paper can simplify cleanup and prevent sticking. For those who venture into bread-making, a stand mixer with a dough hook attachment can be a game-changer, making the kneading process far less labor-intensive.

For beginners, small appliances can greatly enhance efficiency and versatility in the kitchen. An electric hand mixer is invaluable for whipping cream, beating egg whites, and mixing batter. A food processor can handle a multitude of tasks, from chopping vegetables to making dough and pureeing soups. A blender is essential for smoothies, sauces, and soups, while an immersion blender offers convenience for pureeing directly in pots. A rice cooker can simplify the process of cooking perfect rice every time, and a slow cooker allows for hands-off cooking of stews, soups, and roasts.

Cutting boards are fundamental to any kitchen, and having more than one is advisable to prevent cross-contamination. Wooden cutting boards are excellent for vegetables and breads, while plastic or composite boards are better suited for raw meats and seafood due to their non-porous nature and ease of sanitization. Regular cleaning and occasional oiling of wooden boards will maintain their condition and longevity.

Utensils and gadgets play a crucial role in everyday cooking tasks. A set of sturdy wooden spoons, heat-resistant silicone spatulas, and metal tongs are indispensable for stirring, scraping, and flipping. A whisk is essential for emulsifying dressings and whipping ingredients. A box grater and a microplane are necessary for grating cheese, zesting citrus, and mincing garlic. A vegetable peeler, can opener, and kitchen shears round out the list of basic utensils. Investing in good-quality tools that feel comfortable in hand will make cooking more enjoyable and efficient.

Storage solutions are often overlooked but are vital for maintaining an organized and functional kitchen. Airtight containers in various sizes are essential for storing dry goods, leftovers, and prepped ingredients. Glass containers are excellent for their non-reactive nature and transparency, making it easy to see contents. A spice rack or drawer organizer can keep spices accessible and neatly arranged. Proper storage not only extends the shelf life of ingredients but also streamlines the cooking process by keeping everything within easy reach.

Temperature control tools like thermometers are crucial for achieving perfect results in cooking and baking. An instant-read thermometer ensures meats are cooked to the correct doneness, while an oven thermometer verifies that your oven is heating accurately. A candy thermometer is essential for tasks like making caramel or deep-frying. These tools take the guesswork out of cooking, allowing for precision and consistency.

Cleaning tools, though often overlooked, are essential for maintaining a hygienic and efficient kitchen. A good dish rack, scrub brushes, and microfiber cloths are basics for daily cleaning. A high-quality dish soap and a sanitizing solution will keep surfaces and tools clean and safe. Regular maintenance of kitchen equipment, such as descaling coffee makers and sharpening knives, will extend their lifespan and performance.

Learning to use and care for kitchen equipment is as important as the equipment itself. Taking the time to understand proper techniques, such as knife skills and cooking methods, will maximize the potential of your tools. Regular maintenance, including sharpening knives, seasoning cast iron, and cleaning appliances, ensures longevity and reliability.

While it may be tempting to buy every gadget and appliance available, focusing on fundamental, high-quality equipment will serve you better in the long run. Prioritize items that offer versatility and durability, and gradually expand your collection as you discover specific needs and preferences in your cooking journey.

# Key Ingredients in Modern Cuisine

Cooking has evolved significantly over the past few decades, influenced by global culinary trends, innovative techniques, and a growing appreciation for diverse flavors. Modern cuisine, with its emphasis on fresh, high-quality ingredients, reflects a blend of tradition and innovation. Understanding the key ingredients that define contemporary cooking can elevate your culinary creations and expand your repertoire. This chapter explores essential ingredients that have become staples in modern kitchens, offering insights into their selection, use, and unique contributions to various dishes.

Olive oil, often hailed as liquid gold, is a cornerstone of modern cuisine. Its versatility and health benefits make it indispensable in cooking and finishing dishes. Extra virgin olive oil, with its robust flavor and high antioxidant content, is ideal for dressings, marinades, and drizzling over finished dishes. For cooking at higher temperatures, regular olive oil with a higher smoke point is preferable. The quality of olive oil can vary significantly, so selecting a reputable brand and tasting different varieties will help identify the best options for your kitchen.

Avocado, once considered exotic, has become a beloved ingredient in modern kitchens worldwide. Its creamy texture and mild flavor make it a versatile addition to both savory and sweet dishes. Rich in healthy fats, avocados are perfect for making guacamole, spreading on toast, or adding to salads and smoothies. Their nutritional profile, including high levels of potassium, fiber, and vitamins, contributes to their popularity. When selecting avocados, look for those that yield slightly to gentle pressure and have a uniform color.

Quinoa, an ancient grain from South America, has gained prominence as a superfood in modern cuisine. Its high protein content, including all nine essential amino acids, makes it a complete protein source, ideal for vegetarians and vegans. Quinoa's nutty flavor and fluffy texture make it a versatile base for salads, bowls, and side dishes. It's essential to rinse quinoa thoroughly before cooking to remove its natural coating, saponin, which can impart a bitter taste. Experimenting with different cooking methods, such as toasting before boiling, can enhance its flavor and texture.

Coconut milk and coconut oil have become staples in modern kitchens, celebrated for their rich flavor and versatility. Coconut milk, made by blending coconut meat with water, is a key ingredient in many Southeast Asian and Caribbean dishes. Its creamy texture and subtle sweetness enhance curries, soups, and desserts. Coconut oil, with its high smoke point and distinct flavor, is excellent for frying, baking, and sautéing. While both coconut milk and oil are high in saturated fats, they contain medium-chain triglycerides (MCTs), which may offer health benefits.

Sriracha, a Thai chili sauce, has taken the culinary world by storm with its perfect balance of heat, sweetness, and tanginess. Made from sun-ripened chili peppers, garlic, vinegar, sugar, and salt, Sriracha adds a spicy kick to a wide range of dishes. Its versatility extends beyond traditional Asian cuisine; it can be used in marinades, sauces, soups, and even cocktails. The popularity of Sriracha has inspired numerous variations and products, from Sriracha-infused snacks to condiments.

Miso, a fermented soybean paste, is a cornerstone of Japanese cuisine that has found a place in modern kitchens worldwide. Its umami-rich flavor adds depth to soups, dressings, marinades, and glazes. Miso comes in various types, ranging from the mild and sweet white miso to the robust and salty red miso. Incorporating miso into your cooking can enhance the flavor profile of both traditional and contemporary dishes. When using miso, it's essential to avoid boiling it to preserve its beneficial probiotics and complex flavors.

Chia seeds, tiny black or white seeds from the Salvia hispanica plant, have become a popular ingredient in health-conscious kitchens. Packed with omega-3 fatty acids, fiber, and antioxidants, chia seeds offer numerous health benefits. They can absorb up to 12 times their weight in liquid, forming a gel-like consistency, making them ideal for puddings, smoothies, and as an egg substitute in baking. Their mild flavor allows them to blend seamlessly into both sweet and savory dishes.

Turmeric, a bright yellow spice from the ginger family, has gained recognition for its anti-inflammatory properties and vibrant color. Its warm, earthy flavor is a staple in Indian and Middle Eastern cuisines, often used in curries, rice dishes, and soups. Turmeric's active compound, curcumin, is renowned for its potential health benefits, including reducing inflammation and boosting immunity. Pairing turmeric with black pepper enhances the absorption of curcumin, making it more effective.

Kale, a leafy green vegetable, has seen a surge in popularity due to its impressive nutritional profile. Rich in vitamins A, C, and K, as well as antioxidants and fiber, kale is a versatile ingredient in modern cuisine. It can be used in salads, soups, smoothies, and as a base for green juices. Massaging kale with a bit of olive oil and salt can soften its tough leaves, making it more palatable for raw preparations. Baking kale into chips offers a healthy alternative to traditional snacks.

Tahini, a paste made from ground sesame seeds, is a staple in Middle Eastern and Mediterranean cuisines. Its rich, nutty flavor and creamy texture make it a versatile ingredient in both savory and sweet dishes. Tahini is a key component of hummus and baba ghanoush, and can also be used in dressings, sauces, and desserts. High in healthy fats, protein, and minerals, tahini adds nutritional value to a variety of recipes.

Cilantro, also known as coriander, is a herb that adds a fresh, citrusy flavor to many dishes. Its leaves and stems are commonly used in Mexican, Indian, and Southeast Asian cuisines. Cilantro pairs well with lime, garlic, and chili, making it a perfect addition to salsas, salads, and curries. While some people have a genetic aversion to cilantro, those who enjoy its flavor find it an indispensable ingredient in their cooking.

Ginger, a pungent and aromatic root, is a key ingredient in many global cuisines. Its spicy, warming flavor enhances both sweet and savory dishes, from stir-fries and curries to cookies and cakes. Fresh ginger is often preferred for its vibrant taste, while ground ginger offers convenience in baking. Ginger's potential health benefits, including aiding digestion and reducing nausea, contribute to its popularity in modern kitchens.

## The Science Behind Cooking

Cooking, at its core, is a series of chemical reactions and physical changes that transform raw ingredients into delicious meals. Understanding the science behind these processes can elevate your culinary skills and help you achieve consistent, mouthwatering results. This chapter delves into the scientific principles that underpin cooking, offering insights into how heat, molecules, and reactions work together to create the food we love.

When you heat food, you're essentially applying energy to change its molecular structure. This energy can come from various sources, such as an oven, stovetop, or microwave. Different cooking methods apply heat in distinct ways, affecting the texture, flavor, and nutritional content of the food. For instance, boiling involves heating water to 100°C (212°F) to cook food through direct contact with hot water and steam. This method is efficient for cooking vegetables and pasta but can lead to nutrient loss due to leaching. On the other hand, roasting uses dry heat to cook food, often resulting in caramelization and Maillard reactions that enhance flavor and create a pleasing texture.

Caramelization and the Maillard reaction are two critical processes that occur during cooking, contributing to the flavor and color of food. Caramelization happens when sugars in food are heated to high temperatures, causing them to break down and form complex compounds with rich, sweet flavors. This process is responsible for the golden-brown hue of roasted vegetables and the deep color of caramel sauce. The Maillard reaction, named after French chemist Louis-Camille Maillard, involves the reaction between amino acids and reducing sugars. This reaction produces hundreds of different flavor compounds, giving browned meat, toasted bread, and seared seafood their distinctive tastes and aromas.

Proteins in food undergo denaturation and coagulation when exposed to heat. Denaturation refers to the unraveling of protein molecules, which occurs when proteins are heated or exposed to acidic conditions. This process is evident when you cook an egg; the clear egg white turns opaque as the proteins denature. Coagulation follows denaturation, where the unraveled protein molecules form new bonds and create a solid structure. This transformation is crucial for achieving the desired texture in dishes like custards, quiches, and soufflés.

Fats play a significant role in cooking, influencing flavor, texture, and mouthfeel. They can act as a medium for heat transfer, as seen in frying, where hot oil cooks food quickly and evenly. Fats also contribute to the tenderness and moisture of baked goods by interfering with gluten formation in doughs. Additionally, fats can emulsify, creating stable mixtures of oil and water. Emulsification is essential in making mayonnaise, hollandaise sauce, and vinaigrettes, where the oil is dispersed in a continuous phase of water or vinegar.

Starches and sugars in food undergo gelatinization and crystallization, processes that are crucial for texture and structure. Gelatinization occurs when starch granules absorb water and swell upon heating, thickening the mixture. This process is fundamental in making sauces, gravies, and puddings. Crystallization, on the other hand, involves the formation of solid crystals from a supersaturated solution. This process is essential in candy-making, where controlling crystallization determines the final texture of the confection.

Acids and bases significantly affect the flavor, texture, and color of food. Acids, such as lemon juice or vinegar, can tenderize meat by breaking down muscle fibers and connective tissue. They also enhance flavors and preserve the vibrant color of fruits and vegetables. Bases, like baking soda, are often used in baking to leaven doughs and batters. When combined with an acid, baking soda releases carbon dioxide gas, causing the mixture to rise and become light and fluffy.

Enzymes are biological catalysts that speed up chemical reactions in food. They play a vital role in fermentation, where microorganisms like yeast and bacteria convert sugars into alcohol, carbon dioxide, and other compounds. Fermentation is the backbone of many culinary traditions, producing bread, beer, wine, cheese, and yogurt. Enzymes also influence the ripening of fruits and vegetables, the tenderizing of meat through marination, and the browning of cut apples and potatoes.

Water content in food affects its texture, flavor, and cooking behavior. Foods with high water content, such as fruits and vegetables, tend to cook quickly and can become mushy if overcooked. Conversely, foods with low water content, like nuts and seeds, require longer cooking times and can become dry if not adequately hydrated. Understanding the water content of ingredients helps in selecting the appropriate cooking method and achieving the desired outcome.

Heat transfer methods—conduction, convection, and radiation—play a crucial role in cooking. Conduction involves direct transfer of heat through contact, such as when a steak sizzles on a hot pan. Convection occurs when heat is transferred through a fluid, like air or water, as seen in baking or boiling. Radiation involves the transfer of heat through electromagnetic waves, as in grilling or broiling. Each method has its advantages and is suitable for different types of food and desired results.

Cooking times and temperatures are critical factors that influence the safety and quality of food. Undercooking can leave harmful bacteria and pathogens in food, posing health risks. Overcooking, on the other hand, can lead to nutrient loss and undesirable textures. Using a food thermometer to monitor internal temperatures ensures that meat, poultry, and seafood are cooked to safe levels. Understanding the science of time and temperature control helps achieve perfect doneness and optimal flavor.

Seasoning and flavor development involve more than just adding salt and pepper. The interaction of various ingredients and cooking methods creates complex flavor profiles. Seasoning at different stages of cooking can enhance the depth of flavor. For instance, salting meat before cooking helps to draw out moisture and create a flavorful crust, while adding herbs and spices at the end preserves their aromatic qualities. Balancing flavors—sweet, salty, sour, bitter, and umami—is essential for creating harmonious and satisfying dishes.

The physical and chemical properties of ingredients determine their behavior during cooking. Understanding these properties allows for better ingredient selection and substitution. For example, knowing that acidic ingredients can curdle dairy helps prevent culinary mishaps, while recognizing the binding properties of eggs can guide you in making custards and emulsions. Experimenting with different ingredients and techniques expands your culinary knowledge and creativity.

# Chapter 2

# Sous Vide Cooking

## Basics of Sous Vide

Sous vide, a French term meaning "under vacuum," is a cooking method that involves sealing food in airtight bags and immersing them in a water bath maintained at a precise temperature. This technique has gained popularity for its ability to produce consistently cooked, flavorful dishes with minimal effort. Understanding the basics of sous vide can revolutionize how you cook and elevate your culinary creations.

The sous vide process begins with selecting the appropriate equipment. A sous vide immersion circulator is essential, as it heats and circulates the water to maintain a consistent temperature. High-quality vacuum sealers are also crucial for removing air from the bags, ensuring even cooking and preventing the bags from floating. If a vacuum sealer is not available, reusable silicone bags with water displacement methods can be used as an alternative.

Temperature control is the cornerstone of sous vide cooking. By setting the water bath to the desired final cooking temperature, you can achieve precise doneness without the risk of overcooking. For example, cooking a steak at 130°F (54.4°C) will result in a perfectly medium-rare steak, retaining its juiciness and tenderness. The low and slow nature of sous vide cooking allows for uniform heat distribution, eliminating the common problem of unevenly cooked food.

Seasoning plays a vital role in sous vide cooking. Since the food is sealed in bags, the flavors intensify as they cannot escape during the cooking process. Simple seasonings like salt, pepper, garlic, and herbs are often sufficient to enhance the natural taste of the ingredients. However, you can experiment with marinades and spice rubs to infuse additional flavors. It's important to note that certain seasonings, such as raw garlic, can become overpowering during long cooking times, so using powdered garlic or briefly sautéing fresh garlic before sealing the bag can help balance the flavors.

Timing is another critical factor in sous vide cooking. While the precise temperature ensures perfect doneness, the cooking time affects the texture. Most proteins, such as beef, pork, chicken, and fish, benefit from longer cooking times, which allow the collagen in the meat to break down, resulting in tender, melt-in-your-mouth dishes. For instance, cooking a pork shoulder at 165°F (73.9°C) for 24 hours will produce succulent, pull-apart meat. Vegetables, on the other hand, require shorter cooking times to retain their crispness and vibrant color.

Once the food is cooked sous vide, finishing techniques are employed to enhance its appearance and flavor. Searing, grilling, or broiling the food after sous vide cooking adds a desirable crust and caramelization, which contribute to the overall taste and presentation. A hot pan with a high smoke point oil or a blowtorch can create the Maillard reaction, giving the food a beautiful brown color and complex flavors. It's essential to pat the food dry before searing to achieve the best results and prevent steaming.

Sous vide is not limited to proteins and vegetables; it can also be used for eggs, desserts, and infusions. Eggs are particularly well-suited for sous vide due to their delicate nature. Cooking eggs at 145°F (62.8°C) for about an hour produces a custard-like texture, perfect for poached eggs or crème brûlée. Desserts, such as cheesecakes and custards, benefit from the precise temperature control, ensuring a smooth and creamy consistency without the risk of curdling. Infusions, like flavored oils, syrups, and spirits, can be created by gently heating the ingredients in a sous vide bath, extracting flavors without boiling or scorching.

When cooking sous vide, it's essential to follow food safety guidelines to ensure the health and safety of your dishes. While the precise temperature control of sous vide cooking minimizes the risk of overcooking, it also means that food is cooked at relatively low temperatures for extended periods. This can create an environment where harmful bacteria can thrive if not properly managed. Always ensure that the food is vacuum-sealed correctly, and maintain the water bath at the recommended temperature for the appropriate duration to pasteurize the food. For example, cooking chicken at 165°F (73.9°C) for at least one hour ensures that it is safe to eat.

Sous vide can also be a time-saving technique for meal prep and entertaining. By cooking food sous vide ahead of time and storing it in the refrigerator or freezer, you can quickly finish and serve dishes with minimal effort. This is particularly useful for busy weeknights or when hosting dinner parties, allowing you to spend more time with your guests rather than being tied to the kitchen. Vacuum-sealed bags also make it easy to portion and store food, reducing waste and maintaining freshness.

One of the most significant advantages of sous vide cooking is its ability to achieve consistent results every time. Traditional cooking methods often involve guesswork and constant monitoring to avoid overcooking or undercooking. With sous vide, the precise temperature control removes the uncertainty, allowing you to replicate your favorite dishes with confidence. This consistency is particularly beneficial for home cooks and professional chefs alike, ensuring that every meal is cooked to perfection.

Experimentation is a key aspect of mastering sous vide cooking. The technique's versatility allows you to try new flavor combinations, cooking times, and temperatures to discover your preferred results. For instance, you can experiment with different herbs and spices, or try cooking proteins at varying temperatures to achieve different textures. Documenting your experiments and results can help you refine your techniques and build a repertoire of go-to recipes.

Sous vide cooking has also gained popularity in the realm of molecular gastronomy, where chefs use scientific principles to create innovative and visually stunning dishes. By combining sous vide with other modernist techniques, such as spherification, foams, and gels, you can create unique dining experiences that push the boundaries of traditional cooking. While these techniques may seem advanced, they are accessible to home cooks with the right equipment and a willingness to experiment.

The environmental impact of sous vide cooking is another consideration for the conscientious cook. While the technique itself is energy-efficient compared to traditional oven or stovetop cooking, the use of plastic bags for vacuum sealing raises concerns about waste. To mitigate this, consider using reusable silicone bags or seeking out biodegradable vacuum-seal bags. Additionally, being mindful of portion sizes and avoiding over-preparation can help reduce food waste.

## Equipment and Setup

Embarking on any culinary adventure requires the right tools and a well-organized setup. When it comes to sous vide cooking, having the proper equipment is paramount for achieving precise and consistent results. Understanding the various components and how they work together will set you up for success in this innovative cooking method.

At the heart of sous vide cooking lies the immersion circulator. This device is responsible for heating the water to a precise temperature and maintaining it throughout the cooking process. Immersion circulators come in various models, ranging from compact units designed for home kitchens to more robust versions suited for professional settings. When choosing an immersion circulator, consider factors such as temperature range, ease of use, and durability. A reliable circulator should offer accurate temperature control, preferably within 0.1 degrees, to ensure perfect doneness every time. Additionally, look for features like a digital display, timer, and Wi-Fi or Bluetooth connectivity for remote monitoring and control.

Next, you'll need a suitable container to hold the water bath. While a large pot or heat-resistant plastic container can suffice for smaller batches, investing in a dedicated sous vide container with a lid offers several advantages. These containers are designed to minimize heat loss and evaporation, which is particularly beneficial for longer cooking times. Some models also come with racks or dividers to keep the food bags submerged and evenly spaced, ensuring uniform cooking. When selecting a container, opt for one that is deep enough to fully submerge the immersion circulator and the food bags without overcrowding.

Vacuum sealing is a crucial step in sous vide cooking, as it removes air from the bags, allowing for efficient heat transfer and preventing the bags from floating. A good vacuum sealer is an invaluable tool, ensuring a tight seal and preserving the quality of the ingredients. Chamber vacuum sealers are ideal for both liquids and solids, providing a secure seal without the risk of liquid being sucked into the machine. However, they tend to be bulkier and more expensive. For home use, an external vacuum sealer is a more practical option, offering a balance between performance and cost. If a vacuum sealer is not available, reusable silicone bags with a water displacement method can be an effective alternative. Simply place the ingredients in the bag, seal it partially, and submerge it in water to push out the air before sealing it completely.

Cooking racks and weights are additional accessories that can enhance your sous vide setup. Cooking racks help organize the bags in the water bath, preventing them from overlapping and ensuring even water circulation. Weights or clips can be used to keep the bags fully submerged, especially when dealing with buoyant ingredients. These tools contribute to consistent cooking results by maintaining proper bag positioning and water flow.

A key aspect of sous vide cooking is precise temperature control, and a reliable thermometer is essential for verifying the accuracy of your immersion circulator. Instant-read digital thermometers are quick and easy to use, allowing you to double-check the water temperature and the internal temperature of the food. This is particularly important when cooking for extended periods, as even slight deviations in temperature can affect the final texture and safety of the dish.

In addition to the core equipment, having a well-organized kitchen setup can streamline your sous vide cooking process. Designate a specific area for your sous vide equipment, including the immersion circulator, vacuum sealer, and containers. Keep frequently used tools, such as tongs, thermometers, and bag clips, within easy reach. Organizing your workspace not only improves efficiency but also reduces the risk of cross-contamination and ensures a smooth cooking experience.

Water quality is another consideration when setting up your sous vide station. Using clean, filtered water helps maintain the longevity of your equipment by preventing mineral buildup and ensuring consistent heating. Some circulators come with built-in filtration systems, but using filtered water from the start can further enhance performance and reduce maintenance.

Properly calibrating your equipment is essential for achieving accurate and reliable results. Periodically check the accuracy of your immersion circulator and thermometer against a known standard, such as a certified reference thermometer. This practice ensures that your devices are functioning correctly and that you can trust the displayed temperatures. Calibration is particularly important for professional kitchens, where precise temperature control is critical for food safety and consistency.

Maintaining your sous vide equipment is crucial for long-term performance and safety. Regularly clean the immersion circulator, paying close attention to the heating element and any removable parts. Follow the manufacturer's guidelines for descaling the circulator to prevent mineral buildup, which can affect heating efficiency. Vacuum sealers also require routine maintenance, such as cleaning the sealing bar and replacing the sealing strip as needed. Proper care and maintenance not only extend the lifespan of your equipment but also ensure safe and reliable operation.

Safety considerations are paramount when setting up your sous vide station. Always use a heat-resistant surface for your water bath container and ensure that the immersion circulator is securely attached. Avoid

using containers that are too shallow, as they can lead
to spills and accidents. Keep electrical components
away from water and follow the manufacturer's safety
instructions for all equipment. Additionally, be
mindful of food safety guidelines, such as cooking at
appropriate temperatures and times to pasteurize the
food and prevent bacterial growth.

## Temperature and Timing Charts

Mastering sous vide cooking hinges on a clear
understanding of temperature and timing. These two
elements are the backbone of achieving desired
textures and flavors in your food. Precision in both is
what sets sous vide apart from other cooking
methods. By adhering to accurate temperature and
timing charts, you can ensure consistent and
exceptional results every time you cook.

When cooking sous vide, temperature control is
crucial. It's what allows for the precise doneness of
food, whether you're preparing a tender steak,
succulent chicken breast, or perfectly cooked
vegetables. The key here is to know the optimal
temperatures for different types of food and their
desired doneness levels. For example, a medium-rare
steak is typically cooked at 129°F (54°C), while a
medium steak would be at 135°F (57°C). Chicken
breasts reach their perfect juiciness at 140°F (60°C),
ensuring they are cooked through but still moist.

Equally important is the cooking time, which can vary
significantly depending on the type and cut of food, as
well as its thickness. Timing affects not only the safety
of the food but also its texture. For instance, cooking a

1-inch thick steak at 129°F (54°C) for one to two hours will result in a tender, medium-rare piece of meat. However, extending the cooking time to three to four hours can break down more connective tissue, leading to an even softer texture. Understanding these nuances allows you to tailor the cooking process to your preferences.

For vegetables, the balance between temperature and time is slightly different. Since they lack the connective tissues found in meats, vegetables require higher temperatures to achieve the desired texture. For example, carrots can be cooked at 183°F (84°C) for about an hour to achieve a tender yet slightly firm consistency. Asparagus, on the other hand, benefits from a shorter cooking time at 185°F (85°C) for around 10 minutes, preserving its vibrant color and crispness.

Eggs are another category where sous vide shines, offering precision that traditional methods can't match. Soft-boiled eggs are typically cooked at 145°F (63°C) for about 45 minutes, resulting in a perfectly set white and a creamy yolk. For the ultimate poached egg, cooking at 167°F (75°C) for 13 minutes delivers a tender white and a runny yolk, ready to top your avocado toast or salad.

To simplify your sous vide cooking, it's helpful to reference detailed temperature and timing charts. These charts serve as a reliable guide, especially when experimenting with new ingredients or techniques. For meats, they typically outline various doneness levels, from rare to well-done, along with corresponding temperatures and recommended cooking times. For example, a pork chop can be cooked to medium at 140°F (60°C) for one to four hours, ensuring it's safe to eat while maintaining its juiciness.

Proteins such as fish and seafood require careful attention to both temperature and time due to their delicate nature. Salmon, for instance, is often cooked at 122°F (50°C) for 30 to 45 minutes, resulting in a buttery texture that melts in your mouth. Shrimp are best cooked at 135°F (57°C) for 15 to 30 minutes to maintain their firm, juicy texture without becoming rubbery.

Understanding the science behind sous vide can also enhance your cooking skills. The concept of pasteurization plays a significant role in determining safe cooking temperatures and times. Pasteurization involves holding food at a specific temperature for a certain period to kill harmful bacteria without compromising quality. For instance, cooking chicken breast at 140°F (60°C) for at least 1 hour and 30 minutes achieves pasteurization, making it safe to consume while keeping it tender and moist.

Another advantage of sous vide is its ability to tenderize tougher cuts of meat. Cuts like beef brisket or short ribs, which are traditionally braised for several hours, can be cooked sous vide for an extended period at a lower temperature to achieve similar, if not better, results. For example, beef brisket can be cooked at 155°F (68°C) for 24 to 36 hours, resulting in a tender, flavorful piece of meat that retains its juices and structure.

Using a precise thermometer is essential for monitoring and maintaining the correct temperature throughout the cooking process. While most immersion circulators are highly accurate, it's always a good idea to double-check with an instant-read thermometer, especially when cooking for extended periods. This practice ensures that the water bath remains at the target temperature, providing consistent results.

Maintaining a log of your sous vide experiments can be incredibly beneficial, particularly when adjusting temperatures and times to suit your preferences. Documenting the details of each cook, including the type of food, thickness, temperature, and duration, allows you to refine your methods and build a personalized reference guide. This practice not only helps in achieving consistent results but also fosters a deeper understanding of how different variables affect the outcome.

In addition to meat, vegetables, and seafood, sous vide is an excellent method for preparing desserts. Custards, for instance, benefit from the precise temperature control that prevents curdling. Cooking a classic crème brûlée at 179°F (82°C) for one hour yields a smooth, creamy texture that's difficult to achieve with traditional baking methods. Similarly, tempering chocolate at specific temperatures ensures a glossy finish with a satisfying snap, ideal for confections and decorations.

When planning a sous vide meal, consider the overall timing and coordination of different dishes. Since sous vide allows for precise holding times without overcooking, you can prepare multiple components in advance and finish them just before serving. This flexibility is particularly useful for entertaining, as it allows you to focus on presentation and plating without the stress of last-minute cooking.

Sous vide cooking also offers opportunities for creative culinary techniques, such as infusions and emulsions. By controlling the temperature, you can infuse flavors into oils, spirits, or syrups with precision. For instance, infusing olive oil with herbs at 131°F (55°C) for a few hours yields a flavorful condiment for drizzling over dishes. Similarly, creating stable emulsions for sauces or dressings is more manageable with the consistent heat provided by sous vide.

## Sous Vide Techniques for Meat and Poultry

Sous vide cooking has revolutionized the way we prepare meat and poultry, offering unprecedented control over temperature and time to achieve perfect results. This technique immerses vacuum-sealed food in a precisely heated water bath, allowing for uniform cooking and optimal texture. Whether you're a home cook or a professional chef, mastering sous vide techniques for meat and poultry can elevate your culinary skills and ensure consistently delicious meals.

The process begins with selecting high-quality cuts of meat and poultry. Freshness is critical, as sous vide cooking preserves and enhances the natural flavors and textures of the ingredients. For beef, popular cuts include ribeye, tenderloin, and sirloin, while chicken breasts and thighs are staples for poultry. Each cut requires specific temperatures and cooking times to achieve the desired doneness and tenderness.

Seasoning is the next crucial step. Since sous vide cooking intensifies flavors, it's essential to season meat and poultry well before sealing. Simple ingredients like salt, pepper, garlic, and fresh herbs can provide a robust flavor base. Marinating the meat beforehand can also infuse additional flavors. For example, marinate a chicken breast with lemon juice, rosemary, and olive oil for a few hours to achieve a vibrant, aromatic result.

Once seasoned, the meat or poultry is placed in a vacuum-seal bag. Removing as much air as possible from the bag is crucial for efficient heat transfer and even cooking. A vacuum sealer is ideal for this purpose, but the water displacement method can also be effective. This involves sealing the bag almost completely, then slowly submerging it in water to push out any remaining air before sealing it entirely.

Setting the correct temperature and cooking time is where the magic of sous vide truly shines. For a medium-rare steak, set the water bath to 129°F (54°C) and cook for one to two hours. This precise temperature ensures the steak is evenly cooked from edge to edge, with a perfect pink center. For chicken breasts, a temperature of 140°F (60°C) for one to two hours results in incredibly juicy and tender meat. The lower cooking temperature compared to traditional methods prevents the chicken from drying out, a common issue when using higher heat.

Cooking times can vary based on the thickness of the meat. Thicker cuts require longer cooking times to ensure the heat penetrates to the center. For instance, a 2-inch thick steak may need up to four hours to cook thoroughly, while a thinner 1-inch steak might only need one hour. The beauty of sous vide is its flexibility; leaving the meat in the water bath for an extra hour or two won't lead to overcooking, thanks to the precise temperature control.

After the sous vide cooking process, meat and poultry often lack the appealing caramelization that comes from traditional high-heat cooking methods. This is where finishing techniques come into play. Quickly searing the meat in a hot skillet with a bit of oil or butter can create a beautiful crust and add complex flavors. For steaks, aim to sear each side for about 30 seconds to a minute, ensuring the pan is hot enough to develop a deep brown crust without overcooking the interior.

Grilling is another excellent finishing method, particularly for poultry. A quick turn on a hot grill can impart a smoky flavor and attractive grill marks. It's essential to keep the grilling time short to preserve the juiciness achieved through sous vide. For chicken breasts, a minute or two on each side is usually sufficient.

Resting the meat after searing is an important step that allows the juices to redistribute, ensuring a moist and flavorful result. Even though the sous vide process minimizes juice loss, resting the meat for a few minutes before slicing can further enhance the final texture and taste. For thicker cuts of beef, a five to ten-minute rest period is ideal, while poultry can rest for about five minutes.

Sous vide cooking also offers unique opportunities to experiment with different flavors and techniques. Infusing the vacuum-seal bag with aromatics like fresh herbs, citrus zest, or even a splash of wine can enhance the flavor profile of the meat. Adding a pat of compound butter made with garlic and herbs before sealing the bag can create a rich, luxurious finish.

When it comes to tougher cuts of meat, sous vide excels at tenderizing while maintaining flavor. Cuts like beef brisket, short ribs, or pork shoulder, which traditionally require long braising times, can be cooked sous vide at lower temperatures for extended periods to achieve incredible tenderness. For example, cooking beef short ribs at 144°F (62°C) for 48 hours results in meat that is meltingly tender yet still retains its structure and flavor.

Safety is a key consideration when cooking meat and poultry sous vide. Ensuring that food is cooked to the appropriate temperatures for pasteurization is crucial to eliminate harmful bacteria. For poultry, maintaining a temperature of at least 140°F (60°C) for a sufficient time ensures both safety and optimal texture. Similarly, for ground meats, which are more prone to bacterial contamination, reaching a temperature of 160°F (71°C) is essential.

Sous vide cooking is not just about achieving perfect doneness; it's also about enhancing the overall dining experience. The consistency and precision offered by this method allow for greater creativity and confidence in the kitchen. Imagine serving a perfectly cooked steak with a side of sous vide carrots, each element precisely timed and executed for a harmonious and delectable meal.

For those new to sous vide, starting with basic cuts and simple seasonings can build confidence and understanding of the process. Gradually experimenting with different cuts, marinades, and finishing techniques can expand your repertoire and showcase the versatility of sous vide cooking.

Moreover, sous vide allows for efficient meal planning and preparation. Vacuum-sealed meat and poultry can be cooked in advance, then quickly seared or grilled before serving. This approach is particularly useful for entertaining, as it reduces last-minute cooking stress and ensures consistently excellent results.

## Advanced Sous Vide Recipes

Experimenting with advanced sous vide recipes can elevate your culinary skills and unlock new flavors and textures in your dishes. This method, known for its precision and consistency, allows you to explore complex flavors and unconventional ingredients, pushing the boundaries of traditional cooking. With an understanding of sous vide basics, you can now delve into more sophisticated recipes that will impress even the most discerning palates.

One of the most fascinating aspects of advanced sous vide cooking is the ability to create multi-component dishes that require precise timing and temperature control. Take, for example, a sous vide duck breast with a cherry port reduction. To achieve the perfect balance of flavors and textures, start by preparing a spice rub for the duck. Combine ground coriander, fennel seeds, black pepper, and sea salt, then generously coat the duck breasts. Seal the duck in vacuum bags and cook in a water bath set to 135°F (57°C) for two hours. This temperature ensures a tender, medium-rare result.

While the duck cooks, prepare the cherry port reduction. In a saucepan, combine pitted cherries, port wine, balsamic vinegar, and a touch of honey. Simmer this mixture until it reduces to a thick, glossy sauce. Once the duck is done, pat it dry and sear it skin-side down in a hot skillet until the skin is crispy and golden. Serve the duck breast sliced, drizzled with the cherry port reduction, and paired with sous vide asparagus or a creamy parsnip purée.

Sous vide also excels in the preparation of seafood, allowing you to achieve delicate textures and vibrant flavors that are difficult to replicate with traditional cooking methods. Consider a sous vide lobster tail with herb butter. Begin by splitting the lobster tails in half and removing the meat from the shells. Season the lobster meat with salt, pepper, and a squeeze of lemon juice before sealing it in a vacuum bag with a generous dollop of herb butter made from softened butter, minced garlic, chopped parsley, and tarragon. Cook the lobster in a water bath set to 135°F (57°C) for 45 minutes. The result is succulent, perfectly cooked lobster that retains its natural sweetness and pairs beautifully with a light, crisp white wine.

For a more elaborate dish, try sous vide lamb shank with a red wine reduction. This recipe involves a longer cook time, but the results are well worth the wait. Season the lamb shanks with salt, pepper, and a blend of rosemary, thyme, and garlic. Seal the shanks in vacuum bags and cook them in a water bath set to

165°F (74°C) for 24 hours. The extended cooking time at this temperature breaks down the tough connective tissue, resulting in meltingly tender meat.

While the lamb shanks cook, prepare the red wine reduction. In a large saucepan, sauté diced onions, carrots, and celery until they are soft and caramelized. Add a bottle of red wine, beef stock, tomato paste, and a bouquet garni of fresh herbs. Simmer this mixture until it reduces by half, then strain out the solids. Once the lamb shanks are done, sear them in a hot skillet to develop a rich, caramelized crust. Serve the lamb shanks with the red wine reduction, accompanied by creamy mashed potatoes or a rustic white bean purée.

Advanced sous vide recipes also provide an excellent opportunity to experiment with desserts, leveraging the precise temperature control to achieve perfect textures. A sous vide crème brûlée is a prime example. Prepare the custard base by whisking together egg yolks, sugar, and vanilla extract, then gradually add warm heavy cream. Strain the mixture to remove any air bubbles and pour it into small Mason jars. Seal the jars and cook them in a water bath set to 179°F (82°C) for one hour. Once the custards are set, chill them in the refrigerator. Just before serving, sprinkle a thin layer of sugar over each custard and use a kitchen torch to caramelize the sugar, creating a crisp, glassy crust.

Another delightful dessert to explore is sous vide poached pears with spiced red wine. Peel and core firm, ripe pears, then place them in vacuum bags with a spiced red wine mixture made from red wine, cinnamon sticks, star anise, and a touch of honey.

Cook the pears in a water bath set to 175°F (80°C) for two hours. The result is tender, flavorful pears infused with the warm spices and rich wine. Serve the poached pears with a dollop of mascarpone cheese or a scoop of vanilla ice cream for an elegant finish to any meal.

For those looking to push the boundaries further, sous vide can be used to create infused spirits and flavored oils. A sous vide gin infusion, for example, allows you to experiment with different botanical combinations. Combine a high-quality gin with your choice of botanicals—such as juniper berries, coriander seeds, citrus peel, and lavender—in a vacuum-sealed bag. Cook the mixture in a water bath set to 135°F (57°C) for two hours. The result is a uniquely flavored gin that can be used to craft innovative cocktails.

Flavored oils are another area where sous vide shines. Create a garlic and rosemary-infused olive oil by sealing fresh garlic cloves and rosemary sprigs with extra virgin olive oil in a vacuum bag. Cook the oil in a water bath set to 140°F (60°C) for two hours. This gentle infusion process preserves the delicate flavors and aromas, resulting in a versatile oil that can be used for drizzling over salads, grilling vegetables, or finishing meat dishes.

The precision and control offered by sous vide cooking make it an ideal method for creating complex, multi-component dishes that require careful timing and temperature management. By mastering these advanced recipes, you can explore new flavors, textures, and techniques that will elevate your culinary repertoire and impress your guests. Whether you're preparing a sophisticated entrée, an elegant dessert, or experimenting with infused spirits and oils, sous vide offers endless possibilities for culinary creativity and innovation.

# Chapter 3
# Molecular Gastronomy

## Introduction to Molecular Gastronomy

Understanding molecular gastronomy transforms the way we approach cooking. This innovative culinary field combines science and art to create extraordinary dishes that surprise and delight the senses. It's not merely about using fancy techniques; it's about understanding the physical and chemical transformations of ingredients during cooking, which allows chefs to manipulate textures, flavors, and presentations in groundbreaking ways.

The roots of molecular gastronomy can be traced back to the late 1980s when physicist Nicholas Kurti and chemist Hervé This coined the term. They aimed to demystify cooking by explaining the scientific principles behind traditional culinary processes. Their work laid the foundation for a new wave of culinary experimentation that has since captivated chefs and food enthusiasts around the globe.

One of the most common techniques in molecular gastronomy is spherification, a method that encapsulates liquids within a gel-like membrane, creating spheres that burst with flavor when bitten into. This technique, popularized by the legendary chef Ferran Adrià, involves two main chemicals: sodium alginate and calcium chloride. By introducing a liquid containing sodium alginate into a calcium chloride bath, a thin, gel-like film forms around the liquid, creating delicate, caviar-like pearls.

To try spherification at home, you can start with a simple recipe like apple juice caviar. Mix apple juice with sodium alginate and blend until smooth. Allow the mixture to sit to remove air bubbles. Next, prepare a calcium chloride bath. Using a dropper, gently release droplets of the apple juice mixture into the calcium chloride solution. The droplets will instantly form spheres. Rinse them in water to remove any excess calcium chloride and serve as a unique garnish for desserts or cocktails.

Another fascinating technique is gelification, which involves transforming liquids into gels. This method uses gelling agents like agar-agar or gelatin. Agar-agar, derived from seaweed, is particularly popular in molecular gastronomy due to its firm texture and ability to set at room temperature. To create a simple fruit gel, dissolve agar-agar in fruit juice, bring it to a boil, and pour the mixture into molds. Once it cools and sets, you'll have a firm, flavorful gel that can be cut into various shapes and used creatively in dishes.

Foams are another hallmark of molecular gastronomy, adding both visual appeal and light, airy textures to dishes. These are typically created using a whipping siphon, which forces air into a liquid mixture. The liquid can be anything from flavored cream to fruit puree. For example, a basil foam can be a delightful addition to a tomato salad. Blend fresh basil leaves with a bit of water, strain the mixture, and add it to a whipping siphon along with a stabilizer like soy lecithin. Charge the siphon with nitrous oxide, shake well, and dispense the foam directly onto the dish.

One groundbreaking method that has revolutionized the culinary world is sous vide cooking. This technique involves vacuum-sealing food in plastic bags and cooking it in a water bath at precisely controlled temperatures. The result is perfectly cooked food with unparalleled texture and flavor. While sous vide has become mainstream, its roots in molecular gastronomy emphasize the importance of precision and control in achieving culinary excellence.

For instance, a sous vide steak is a prime example of how this technique can transform a simple ingredient. By cooking the steak at 130°F (54°C) for two hours, you ensure that it's evenly cooked from edge to edge while retaining its juices. After the sous vide process, a quick sear in a hot pan creates a perfect crust, combining the best of both worlds: a tender interior and a crispy exterior.

Emulsification is another technique widely used in molecular gastronomy to create smooth, stable mixtures from liquids that typically don't combine, such as oil and water. This process is essential for making sauces and dressings. A classic example is mayonnaise, where egg yolks act as an emulsifier to blend oil and vinegar. Modern chefs take this concept further by using emulsifiers like soy lecithin to create stable, flavorful emulsions in various dishes.

For a modern twist on a classic vinaigrette, try making a raspberry vinaigrette using soy lecithin as an emulsifier. Blend fresh raspberries with vinegar, then slowly add oil while blending to create a stable emulsion. The soy lecithin helps maintain the mixture's consistency, resulting in a vibrant, flavorful dressing that doesn't separate.

Dehydration is a technique that removes moisture from food, concentrating its flavors and altering its texture. This method is often used to create crunchy elements in dishes, like vegetable chips or fruit crisps. Dehydrators are commonly used for this purpose, but a low-temperature oven can also be effective. For example, thinly sliced strawberries can be dehydrated to create a sweet, crunchy garnish for desserts or breakfast dishes.

Nitrogen freezing is another captivating method in molecular gastronomy, utilizing liquid nitrogen to rapidly freeze ingredients. This technique allows chefs to achieve unique textures and presentations. For instance, liquid nitrogen can be used to create ultra-smooth ice creams or to freeze herbs, which can then be crumbled into fine powders for garnishing.

To make a striking frozen dessert, consider trying liquid nitrogen ice cream. Mix a traditional ice cream base with your desired flavors, then slowly add liquid nitrogen while stirring continuously. The rapid freezing process creates an exceptionally smooth texture that's hard to achieve with conventional methods. This technique not only enhances texture but also offers a visually stunning presentation with clouds of nitrogen vapor.

Encapsulation is another intriguing technique where flavors are trapped inside a shell, releasing bursts of taste when consumed. This method is often employed with ingredients like oils, vinegars, or juices. To encapsulate olive oil, for example, mix it with sodium alginate and drop it into a calcium chloride bath, creating small, caviar-like beads that burst with flavor when eaten.

Molecular gastronomy also explores the use of hydrocolloids—substances that form gels with water. These include xanthan gum, carrageenan, and pectin. Xanthan gum, for instance, can thicken sauces without altering their flavor, creating smooth, velvety textures. Carrageenan, derived from seaweed, is used to create firm gels and can even mimic the texture of dairy products, making it a valuable tool for creating vegan dishes.

## Key Techniques Spherification, Gelification, and Emulsification

Mastering the techniques of spherification, gelification, and emulsification opens a world of culinary creativity. These methods, cornerstones of molecular gastronomy, allow chefs to transform ingredients in unexpected ways, creating dishes that tantalize both the palate and the imagination.

Spherification, the process of creating liquid-filled spheres that burst in the mouth, has become an iconic technique in modern cuisine. This method involves two primary chemicals: sodium alginate and calcium chloride. By introducing a sodium alginate solution to a calcium chloride bath, a gel-like membrane forms around the liquid, trapping it inside. The result is a delicate sphere that can encapsulate a variety of flavors, from fruit juices to cocktail ingredients.

Imagine serving a cocktail where each sip includes a burst of encapsulated citrus essence. To create such spheres, start by mixing your chosen liquid, such as lime juice, with sodium alginate. Allow the mixture to sit to remove any air bubbles. Next, prepare a calcium chloride bath by dissolving the calcium chloride in water. Using a dropper, gently release droplets of the lime juice mixture into the bath. Within seconds, the droplets will form spheres. Carefully remove them and rinse in water to eliminate any residual calcium chloride.

Spherification isn't limited to liquids; it can also be applied to semi-solids like purees. For instance, a tomato puree can be spherified and served as a unique garnish for salads, adding both visual appeal and bursts of intense flavor. The key to successful spherification lies in precise measurements and patience, ensuring the mixture has the correct consistency and the spheres form uniformly.

Gelification, another transformative technique, involves turning liquids into gels using gelling agents such as agar-agar, gelatin, or carrageenan. This method can be used to create a wide range of textures, from firm jellies to soft, melt-in-the-mouth gels. Agar-agar, derived from seaweed, is particularly favored in molecular gastronomy due to its ability to set at room temperature and its firm texture.

To experiment with gelification, consider making a fruit gel. Begin by dissolving agar-agar in fruit juice, then bring the mixture to a boil to activate the gelling agent. Pour the hot mixture into molds and allow it to cool. Once set, you can cut the gel into various shapes to complement your dishes. For a more playful approach, pour the mixture into a flat tray to create a sheet of gel, then cut it into ribbons or shapes using cookie cutters.

Gelification can also be used to create layers within a dish, adding both texture and flavor complexity. A layered dessert, like a panna cotta with fruit gel layers, showcases the technique beautifully. Each layer offers a different flavor and texture, making every bite a new experience. The versatility of gelification makes it a valuable tool for any chef looking to innovate in the kitchen.

Emulsification, the process of combining two immiscible liquids like oil and water, is essential for creating smooth, stable mixtures. This technique is crucial in making dressings, sauces, and even some desserts. Traditional emulsifiers include egg yolks and mustard, but modern chefs often use soy lecithin and other stabilizers to achieve perfect emulsions.

A classic example of emulsification is mayonnaise. By gradually whisking oil into egg yolks and vinegar, you create a thick, creamy sauce. The lecithin in the egg yolks acts as an emulsifier, binding the oil and vinegar together. For a twist, try making a flavored mayonnaise by adding ingredients like garlic, herbs, or spices to the basic recipe. The key to successful emulsification is to add the oil slowly and whisk continuously, ensuring the mixture doesn't separate.

Emulsification extends beyond sauces and dressings. It can be used to create light, airy mousses and foams. For instance, a chocolate mousse relies on the emulsification of cream and melted chocolate. By whipping the cream and chocolate together, you create a stable mixture that holds air, resulting in a light, fluffy texture. Emulsification can also be used to create savory foams, adding a modern touch to classic dishes.

To create a basil foam, blend fresh basil leaves with a bit of water, then strain the mixture to obtain a smooth liquid. Add a stabilizer like soy lecithin, then use a whipping siphon to aerate the mixture. The result is a light, flavorful foam that can be used to garnish soups, salads, or main courses. The combination of flavor and texture adds an element of surprise to the dish, enhancing the dining experience.

Each of these techniques—spherification, gelification, and emulsification—offers unique possibilities for creativity in the kitchen. By mastering them, you can transform ordinary ingredients into extraordinary culinary creations. These methods not only enhance the visual appeal of dishes but also add new dimensions of texture and flavor, making every bite a memorable experience.

As you explore these techniques, remember that precision and experimentation are key. Accurate measurements and careful control of conditions are essential for achieving the desired results. Don't be afraid to experiment with different flavors and ingredients, and let your creativity guide you. The world of molecular gastronomy is vast and full of potential, offering endless opportunities to innovate and delight your guests.

These techniques also encourage a deeper understanding of the science behind cooking. By learning how ingredients interact on a molecular level, you gain greater control over the outcomes of your dishes. This knowledge empowers you to push the boundaries of traditional cooking, creating dishes that not only taste amazing but also tell a story and evoke emotion.

Incorporate these techniques into your culinary repertoire, and you'll find yourself looking at ingredients in a whole new light. A simple tomato becomes a canvas for spherification, a fruit juice transforms into a gel, and a basic dressing evolves into an emulsion. The possibilities are limited only by your imagination and willingness to experiment.

# Tools and Ingredients for Molecular Gastronomy

Exploring the realm of molecular gastronomy requires an array of specialized tools and ingredients. These components are the backbone of the inventive techniques that define this culinary field. Understanding their uses and characteristics is essential for anyone eager to delve into the fascinating world where science meets cuisine.

Among the most fundamental tools for molecular gastronomy is the immersion circulator. This device enables precise temperature control, essential for sous-vide cooking, a technique where food is vacuum-sealed and often cooked in a water bath for extended periods. The immersion circulator ensures that the water maintains a consistent temperature, which is crucial for achieving the desired texture and doneness of the food. For example, cooking a steak sous-vide at

130°F (54°C) guarantees a perfect medium-rare result throughout, unlike traditional methods where the outer layers tend to be more well-done than the interior.

Another indispensable tool is the digital scale, which provides the accuracy needed for measuring ingredients in molecular gastronomy. Many techniques, such as spherification and gelification, require precise measurements of chemicals and additives to ensure successful outcomes. A digital scale that measures in grams and milligrams helps ensure that you are using the correct amounts, thus avoiding failed experiments and inconsistent results.

The whipping siphon is also a staple in the molecular gastronomy toolkit. This versatile device uses pressurized gas to create foams, mousses, and even carbonated fruits. By charging the siphon with nitrous oxide, you can infuse liquids with air, creating light and airy textures. For instance, a simple cream can be transformed into a delicate espuma, adding a touch of sophistication to desserts or savory dishes.

On the cutting edge of molecular gastronomy, the anti-griddle offers a unique way to create frozen or semi-frozen ingredients quickly. This tool features a super-cooled metal surface that instantly freezes anything placed on it. Chefs use the anti-griddle to make frozen canapés, cold garnishes, and even novel desserts. Imagine serving a frozen yogurt disk that melts in the mouth, providing a refreshing burst of flavor.

Pipettes and small syringes are essential for precision work, especially in techniques like spherification and creating intricate garnishes. These tools allow for the accurate placement of liquids and gels, ensuring that each component of a dish is exactly where it needs to be. For instance, using a syringe to place tiny dots of flavored gel on a plate can enhance the visual appeal and taste of the dish.

In addition to tools, specific ingredients play a crucial role in molecular gastronomy. Hydrocolloids, such as agar-agar, gelatin, and xanthan gum, are commonly used to manipulate the texture of food. Agar-agar, derived from seaweed, is a vegetarian alternative to gelatin and is used to create firm gels that set at room temperature. Xanthan gum, on the other hand, is a powerful thickening agent that can stabilize emulsions and create smooth, viscous liquids.

Sodium alginate and calcium chloride are pivotal in the spherification process. When sodium alginate is mixed with a flavored liquid and then dropped into a calcium chloride bath, it forms a gel-like membrane around the liquid, creating spheres that burst in the mouth. This technique allows chefs to encapsulate flavors and create visually striking presentations.

Lecithin, a natural emulsifier, is often used to create stable emulsions and foams. Derived from soybeans or egg yolks, lecithin helps combine water and oil-based ingredients, which would typically separate. This property is invaluable in making smooth sauces, dressings, and light, airy foams that enhance the mouthfeel and appearance of dishes.

Another key ingredient is maltodextrin, a carbohydrate derived from starch. Maltodextrin's unique ability to absorb fats makes it useful for creating powdery textures from oily substances. For example, chefs can transform olive oil into a fine powder that melts on the tongue, providing a surprising twist on a familiar flavor.

Liquid nitrogen, while not an ingredient in the traditional sense, is a critical component in molecular gastronomy. This extremely cold substance ($-320°F$ or $-196°C$) is used to flash-freeze ingredients, creating dramatic effects and unique textures. The rapid freezing process preserves the integrity and flavor of the food while allowing for creative presentations. For instance, liquid nitrogen can be used to make ice creams with an incredibly smooth texture or to create stunning frozen garnishes that vaporize upon serving.

Understanding the basic principles behind these tools and ingredients is only the first step. Practical application and experimentation are necessary to master the techniques of molecular gastronomy. Start with simple recipes and gradually incorporate more complex methods as you become comfortable with the tools and ingredients.

For beginners, it's helpful to practice with basic recipes that incorporate one or two molecular gastronomy techniques. For instance, try making a simple fruit caviar using the spherification method. Mix fruit juice with sodium alginate, then carefully drop it into a calcium chloride bath to create small, caviar-like spheres. This exercise will help you understand the properties of the ingredients and the importance of precise measurements.

Once you have a handle on the basics, you can start combining techniques to create more elaborate dishes. For example, you could make a layered dessert that includes a gelified fruit layer, a foam topping, and spherified flavor pearls. The key to success is to understand how each element interacts and complements the others, creating a harmonious and visually appealing dish.

Remember to keep meticulous notes during your experiments. Document the quantities of each ingredient, the temperatures used, and the outcomes of your trials. This practice will help you refine your techniques and replicate successful results. Over time, you'll develop a deeper understanding of how to manipulate textures and flavors to achieve your culinary vision.

Molecular gastronomy is not just about using high-tech equipment and exotic ingredients. It's about enhancing the dining experience by pushing the boundaries of traditional cooking methods. By mastering the tools and ingredients of this innovative field, you can create dishes that are not only delicious but also visually stunning and thought-provoking.

## Safety and Precision in Molecular Cooking

Molecular cooking, with its innovative techniques and scientific approach, offers an exciting frontier for culinary enthusiasts. However, the precision required and the unique ingredients and tools used also introduce potential hazards. Ensuring safety and accuracy in the kitchen is paramount for both the success of your dishes and your well-being. This chapter delves into the essential practices for maintaining safety and precision in molecular cooking.

Precision in molecular cooking begins with meticulous measurement and control. The techniques often involve chemicals and processes that react in very specific ways, necessitating exact quantities and conditions. A digital scale capable of measuring to the nearest gram or milligram is indispensable. It ensures that your ratios are correct, whether you're measuring sodium alginate for spherification or agar-agar for gelification. Even slight deviations can lead to failed experiments or, worse, unsafe reactions.

Temperature control is another critical aspect of precision. Sous-vide cooking, for instance, relies on maintaining a consistent water bath temperature to achieve perfect results. An immersion circulator is the tool of choice here, allowing you to set and hold precise temperatures. This precision ensures that meats are cooked evenly, retaining moisture and flavor, and that delicate ingredients like eggs reach the exact doneness desired. Investing in a high-quality immersion circulator with reliable temperature accuracy is a wise decision for anyone serious about molecular cooking.

Safety in molecular gastronomy extends beyond accurate measurements and temperature control. Many techniques involve chemicals and ingredients that can be hazardous if mishandled. For example, calcium chloride, used in spherification, can be irritating to the skin and eyes. Always wear gloves and eye protection when handling it and similar substances. Additionally, ensure that your workspace is well-ventilated to avoid inhaling any fine powders or fumes generated during cooking.

Liquid nitrogen, a common tool in molecular gastronomy for flash-freezing and creating dramatic effects, poses significant risks due to its extreme cold. Handling liquid nitrogen requires specialized equipment and strict safety protocols. Always wear insulated gloves and face protection to prevent frostbite and other injuries. Use liquid nitrogen in a well-ventilated area to avoid asphyxiation risks from nitrogen gas displacing oxygen in the air. Proper training in handling and storage is crucial to prevent accidents.

Another essential aspect of safety in molecular cooking is understanding the properties and interactions of the ingredients you're using. Some additives, like sodium alginate and calcium chloride, can react in unexpected ways if combined improperly. Thoroughly research each ingredient and its interactions before experimenting. Reliable sources such as scientific journals, culinary textbooks, and reputable online resources can provide the necessary information to use these ingredients safely and effectively.

Precision also involves the timing of your culinary processes. Many molecular techniques require exact timing to achieve the desired results. For example, in reverse spherification, the sodium alginate mixture must be left in the calcium lactate bath for a specific duration to form a perfect gel sphere. Using a digital timer ensures you adhere to these precise timings, preventing over- or under-formation of the spheres.

Maintaining a clean and organized workspace is vital for both safety and precision. Cross-contamination can occur if residues of one ingredient mix with another, potentially ruining your dish or causing harmful reactions. Clean your tools and surfaces thoroughly between different stages of your cooking process. An organized workspace also helps you keep track of your ingredients and measurements, reducing the risk of mistakes.

Proper storage of ingredients and chemicals is another critical safety measure. Many molecular gastronomy ingredients are sensitive to moisture, light, and temperature. Store them in airtight containers, away from direct sunlight, and in a cool, dry place. Label each container clearly with the ingredient name and its concentration or potency where applicable. This practice not only ensures the longevity of your ingredients but also prevents confusion and potential misuse.

When working with molecular techniques, it's essential to stay informed about the latest safety guidelines and best practices. The culinary field is continuously evolving, and new research can provide insights into safer and more effective ways to use molecular gastronomy techniques. Joining professional culinary organizations, attending workshops, and participating in online forums can help you stay updated and connected with other practitioners in the field.

One often overlooked aspect of safety in molecular cooking is the potential for allergic reactions to new and exotic ingredients. Always be aware of the dietary restrictions and allergies of those who will be consuming your dishes. Clearly label any dishes that contain common allergens like soy lecithin or unusual ingredients that might trigger sensitivities. When in doubt, consult with your diners about their allergies and preferences before experimenting with new recipes.

Precision and safety are also about understanding the limits of your equipment and ingredients. Not all tools are suitable for every task, and using the wrong equipment can lead to accidents or failed dishes. For example, using a standard blender instead of an immersion blender for certain emulsification processes can result in inconsistent textures and potential splattering. Invest in the right tools for the job and ensure you understand their proper use and maintenance.

Documentation plays a crucial role in achieving precision and ensuring safety in molecular cooking. Keep detailed records of your experiments, including the quantities of ingredients used, the timings of each process, and the conditions under which you worked. This practice not only helps you reproduce successful dishes but also allows you to identify and correct mistakes. Over time, these records become an invaluable resource for refining your techniques and expanding your culinary repertoire.

It's also important to consider the environmental impact of your molecular gastronomy practices. Many chemicals and tools used in molecular cooking require responsible disposal and handling. Follow local regulations for disposing of chemical wastes, and consider environmentally friendly alternatives where possible. For instance, using plant-based gelling agents like agar-agar instead of animal-derived gelatin can reduce your environmental footprint.

Incorporating these safety and precision practices into your molecular cooking routine may seem daunting at first, but they quickly become second nature with experience and discipline. The rewards are well worth the effort, as you'll be able to create dishes that are not only innovative and visually stunning but also safe and reliable.

Ultimately, the essence of molecular gastronomy lies in the harmonious blend of creativity, science, and technique. By prioritizing safety and precision in your culinary endeavors, you set the foundation for exploring this exciting field with confidence and success. Whether you're a professional chef or an enthusiastic home cook, these principles guide you towards mastering the art and science of molecular cooking, ensuring that your culinary creations are both groundbreaking and safe.

## Signature Dishes and Recipes

Creating signature dishes and recipes is an exhilarating journey that combines creativity, technique, and a deep understanding of flavors. These dishes often become a defining feature of a chef's repertoire, showcasing their unique style and culinary philosophy. To craft a signature dish, one must consider various elements, from ingredient selection and preparation methods to presentation and storytelling.

The foundation of any signature dish lies in the choice of ingredients. Opting for high-quality, seasonal, and locally sourced ingredients can elevate the flavors and authenticity of your creation. When selecting ingredients, think about how they complement and contrast with each other. Consider their textures, flavors, and colors, ensuring a harmonious balance. For instance, pairing a rich, fatty protein like duck breast with a tart fruit sauce can create a delightful contrast that excites the palate.

Understanding the technical aspects of cooking is crucial for developing a signature dish. Mastery of various cooking techniques allows you to manipulate ingredients to achieve the desired textures and flavors. Techniques such as sous-vide, searing, and emulsification can transform ordinary ingredients into extraordinary components of your dish. Experimenting with these methods helps you discover new possibilities and refine your approach to culinary creation.

Presentation plays a significant role in the appeal of a signature dish. The visual aspect of a dish can entice diners even before they take their first bite. Consider the use of color, shape, and arrangement to create an aesthetically pleasing plate. Utilizing modern plating techniques, such as negative space, height, and symmetry, can enhance the visual impact of your dish. Additionally, incorporating edible garnishes and decorative elements can add a touch of elegance and sophistication.

Storytelling is an often overlooked but essential component of a signature dish. Every dish has a story, whether it's inspired by a personal experience, a cultural tradition, or a specific ingredient's journey. Sharing the story behind your dish can create a deeper connection with your diners, making the experience more memorable. For example, a dish inspired by your grandmother's cooking can evoke nostalgia and warmth, resonating with those who have similar memories.

The process of developing a signature dish involves experimentation and iteration. Start with a concept or idea and build upon it through trial and error. Keep detailed notes of each attempt, documenting the ingredients, techniques, and outcomes. This practice allows you to refine your dish systematically, identifying what works and what needs improvement. Don't be afraid to experiment with unconventional combinations or techniques; innovation often leads to remarkable discoveries.

Consistency is key when it comes to signature dishes. Once you've perfected your recipe, ensure that you can reproduce it with the same quality and precision every time. Standardizing your procedures and measurements helps maintain consistency, whether you're cooking for a small gathering or a large event. Consistency builds trust with your diners, as they know they can expect the same exceptional experience each time they order your signature dish.

To illustrate the process of creating a signature dish, let's take the example of a "Seared Scallops with Citrus Beurre Blanc and Fennel Salad." This dish combines the delicate sweetness of scallops with the bright acidity of citrus and the refreshing crunch of fennel, resulting in a balanced and sophisticated plate.

Start by selecting fresh, high-quality scallops. Look for scallops that are plump, slightly translucent, and have a sweet, briny aroma. Pat them dry with paper towels to remove excess moisture, which helps achieve a perfect sear. Season the scallops with salt and pepper just before cooking.

Heat a skillet over medium-high heat and add a small amount of oil with a high smoke point, such as grapeseed or canola oil. When the oil is shimmering, carefully place the scallops in the skillet, ensuring they are not crowded. Sear the scallops for about 2 minutes on each side until they develop a golden-brown crust and are just opaque in the center. Remove the scallops from the skillet and set them aside.

For the citrus beurre blanc, start by reducing a mixture of white wine, lemon juice, and orange juice in a saucepan over medium heat. Allow the liquid to reduce by half, concentrating the flavors. Lower the heat and gradually whisk in cold, cubed butter, one piece at a time, until the sauce is smooth and emulsified. Season the beurre blanc with salt and a touch of freshly ground white pepper.

To prepare the fennel salad, thinly slice a fresh fennel bulb using a mandoline or sharp knife. Toss the fennel slices with a drizzle of olive oil, a squeeze of lemon juice, and a pinch of salt. The fennel's crisp texture and mild anise flavor provide a refreshing contrast to the rich scallops and buttery sauce.

When plating the dish, place a few seared scallops on each plate. Spoon the citrus beurre blanc around the scallops, allowing it to pool slightly. Arrange a small mound of fennel salad next to the scallops, adding a vibrant green element to the plate. Garnish with fennel fronds or microgreens for an elegant touch.

By focusing on high-quality ingredients, mastering cooking techniques, and paying attention to presentation, you've created a dish that not only delights the senses but also tells a story. The combination of flavors, textures, and visual appeal makes this dish a standout example of a signature recipe.

Signature dishes often evolve over time as you refine your techniques and discover new ingredients. Stay open to inspiration and continue experimenting with different elements. Listening to feedback from diners can also provide valuable insights and help you further enhance your creation. Remember, a signature dish is a reflection of your culinary journey and personal style, so let your creativity and passion shine through in every bite.

# Chapter 4
# Fermentation Techniques

## History and Benefits of Fermentation

Fermentation is an ancient culinary technique that has played a pivotal role in human history. This transformative process, which involves the conversion of carbohydrates to alcohol or organic acids using microorganisms—yeasts, bacteria, or both—has been utilized for thousands of years to preserve food, enhance flavors, and improve nutritional value. Understanding the history and benefits of fermentation provides valuable insights into its enduring significance and how it can be harnessed in modern culinary practices.

The origins of fermentation are deeply rooted in prehistory, long before the advent of written records. Early humans likely discovered fermentation by accident, noticing that certain foods and beverages improved in flavor and longevity after being left to sit for a period. Archaeological evidence suggests that as early as 7000 BCE, people in Jiahu, China, were fermenting a mix of rice, honey, and fruit to create a primitive form of alcohol. Similarly, early Egyptians and Sumerians were brewing beer and baking leavened bread as early as 3000 BCE.

Fermentation spread across cultures and continents, becoming integral to various culinary traditions. In Europe, the ancient Greeks and Romans fermented grapes to produce wine, while in Asia, the Koreans developed kimchi, a fermented vegetable dish, and the Japanese perfected the art of fermenting soybeans to create miso and soy sauce. These practices were not merely about preservation but also about enhancing the sensory qualities of food.

One of the most significant benefits of fermentation is its ability to preserve food. Before the invention of refrigeration, fermentation was a crucial method for extending the shelf life of perishable items. By creating an acidic or alcoholic environment, fermentation inhibits the growth of spoilage-causing bacteria and molds. This preservation method ensured that communities had access to essential nutrients during times of scarcity, such as winter months or long voyages.

Fermentation also enhances the nutritional profile of food. The process breaks down complex carbohydrates, proteins, and fats into simpler, more digestible compounds. For example, in the fermentation of dairy products like yogurt and kefir, lactose is converted into lactic acid, making these products more digestible for individuals with lactose intolerance. Additionally, fermentation can increase the bioavailability of vitamins and minerals. Sauerkraut, a fermented cabbage dish, is rich in vitamin C and beneficial probiotics, which support gut health.

The health benefits of fermented foods extend beyond improved digestion. Fermented foods are a natural source of probiotics, live microorganisms that confer numerous health benefits when consumed in adequate amounts. These beneficial bacteria can help balance the gut microbiome, which plays a crucial role in overall health, including immune function, mental health, and metabolic processes. Regular consumption of fermented foods has been linked to reduced inflammation, enhanced immune response, and even a lower risk of certain chronic diseases.

The flavor development facilitated by fermentation is another compelling advantage. Fermentation introduces complex, nuanced flavors that cannot be achieved through other cooking methods. The umami taste in soy sauce, the tanginess in yogurt, and the deep, earthy flavors in sourdough bread all result from fermentation. These flavors add depth and richness to dishes, elevating them from ordinary to extraordinary.

In addition to preservation, nutrition, and flavor, fermentation has cultural and social significance. Many traditional fermented foods are associated with rituals, festivals, and communal activities. The process of fermenting foods often involves time-honored techniques passed down through generations, fostering a sense of continuity and cultural identity. For example, the making of kimchi in Korea is often a communal activity, with families and neighbors coming together to prepare large batches for the winter months. This practice, known as "kimjang," has been recognized by UNESCO as an Intangible Cultural Heritage of Humanity.

Embracing fermentation in modern culinary practices offers numerous opportunities for creativity and innovation. Home cooks and professional chefs alike can experiment with fermenting various ingredients to create unique flavors and textures. The resurgence of interest in artisanal and homemade foods has led to a renewed appreciation for fermentation, with many individuals exploring the craft of brewing kombucha, making sourdough bread, or fermenting vegetables at home.

For beginners interested in fermentation, starting with simple projects can build confidence and understanding. One accessible entry point is fermenting vegetables, such as making sauerkraut or pickles. These projects require minimal equipment and ingredients, making them ideal for those new to the practice. The basic process involves salting vegetables to draw out moisture, creating a brine that promotes the growth of beneficial bacteria. The vegetables are then left to ferment at room temperature for several days to weeks, depending on the desired level of fermentation.

Safety is a crucial consideration in fermentation. While the process itself creates an environment that inhibits harmful pathogens, it's essential to follow proper guidelines to ensure safe and successful fermentation. Cleanliness is paramount; always use clean equipment and wash your hands thoroughly before handling ingredients. Additionally, using the correct amount of salt and maintaining appropriate temperatures during fermentation are critical for preventing spoilage and ensuring the growth of beneficial microorganisms.

Exploring the diverse world of fermented foods can also deepen one's appreciation for global culinary traditions. Each culture has its own unique fermented foods, reflecting local ingredients, climates, and tastes. From the tangy, spicy kimchi of Korea to the rich, complex flavors of European cheeses, fermented foods offer a window into the culinary heritage of different regions. Trying these foods not only expands one's palate but also fosters a greater understanding of and connection to diverse cultures.

Incorporating fermented foods into daily meals can be both enjoyable and beneficial. Simple additions, such as a spoonful of sauerkraut to a sandwich, a dollop of yogurt to a smoothie, or a splash of kombucha as a refreshing drink, can introduce the benefits of fermentation into your diet. These small changes can contribute to a healthier gut microbiome and overall well-being.

## Tools and Ingredients for Fermentation

Fermentation, the age-old process of transforming food through the action of microorganisms, requires a combination of specific tools and ingredients to achieve successful and safe results. Whether you're a beginner or a seasoned fermenter, understanding the essential equipment and ingredients is crucial for creating a wide range of fermented foods and beverages. This chapter delves into the must-have tools and key ingredients that can help you embark on or refine your fermentation journey.

Starting with tools, the cornerstone of any fermentation project is a reliable fermentation vessel. Glass jars are a popular choice due to their non-reactive nature and the ability to observe the fermentation process. Mason jars, in particular, are ubiquitous in home fermentation, available in various sizes and equipped with tight-fitting lids. When using glass jars, it's essential to leave some headspace to allow for expansion and gas release during fermentation.

For larger batches or continuous fermentation, ceramic crocks are another excellent option. These traditional vessels, often passed down through generations, are ideal for fermenting foods like sauerkraut, kimchi, and pickles. Ceramic crocks are heavy and durable, providing a stable environment for fermentation. Many come with weights and lids designed to keep the fermenting produce submerged in brine, preventing exposure to air and unwanted mold growth.

Stainless steel containers can also be used for fermentation, particularly for brewing kombucha or other beverages. They are non-reactive and easy to clean, but it's important to ensure that any metal parts that come into contact with the ferment are food-grade stainless steel to avoid contamination.

In addition to fermentation vessels, airlocks and fermentation weights are essential tools. Airlocks, available in various designs, allow gases produced during fermentation to escape while preventing outside air from entering the vessel. This helps maintain an anaerobic environment, crucial for the growth of beneficial microorganisms and the prevention of spoilage. Fermentation weights, whether made of glass, ceramic, or food-grade plastic, keep the fermenting produce submerged in brine, which is vital for the success of the process.

A good digital scale is indispensable for accurate measurement of ingredients, particularly salt, which is critical in many fermentation recipes. Salt concentration can significantly impact the outcome of your ferment, so precise measurement is key. Additionally, a mandoline or a sharp knife will help achieve uniform cuts of vegetables, ensuring even fermentation and consistent texture.

Temperature control is another important aspect of fermentation. While some ferments thrive at room temperature, others may require more specific conditions. A simple thermometer can help monitor the ambient temperature, ensuring it stays within the optimal range for your particular fermentation project. For those who live in fluctuating climates, considering a temperature-controlled environment such as a fermentation chamber or a modified cooler can provide more consistent results.

Now, let's turn our attention to the ingredients essential for fermentation. The cornerstone ingredient in most vegetable ferments is salt. Salt not only enhances flavor but also creates an environment conducive to the growth of beneficial bacteria while inhibiting harmful ones. The type of salt used can vary, but non-iodized salts like sea salt, kosher salt, or Himalayan pink salt are recommended. These salts are free from additives that can interfere with the fermentation process.

Water is another critical ingredient. The quality of water used in fermentation can impact the final product. Chlorinated tap water can inhibit the growth of beneficial bacteria, so it's best to use filtered or distilled water. If you must use tap water, let it sit out for 24 hours to allow the chlorine to dissipate or boil it and let it cool before use.

Vegetables, fruits, grains, and dairy are the primary substrates for fermentation. Fresh, high-quality produce is essential for successful fermentation. Organic vegetables free from pesticides and chemicals are ideal, as these substances can hinder the activity of beneficial microorganisms. For dairy ferments like yogurt and kefir, high-quality milk, preferably organic and free from additives, will yield the best results.

Starters, such as whey, yogurt cultures, or specific bacterial cultures, can also be crucial, particularly for dairy and beverage ferments. These starters introduce specific strains of beneficial bacteria to kickstart the fermentation process and ensure a consistent end product. For example, using a SCOBY (Symbiotic Culture of Bacteria and Yeast) is essential for brewing kombucha, while a kefir grain is necessary for making milk kefir.

In some cases, sugar is an essential ingredient, particularly in fermenting beverages like kombucha or water kefir. Sugar serves as a food source for the fermenting microorganisms, which convert it into acids, gases, or alcohol, depending on the ferment. The type of sugar can vary, from white granulated sugar to more natural options like honey or cane sugar, each imparting different flavors and fermentation dynamics.

Spices, herbs, and aromatics can elevate the flavors of your ferments, making them uniquely yours. For instance, caraway seeds are a traditional addition to sauerkraut, while ginger and turmeric can add warmth and complexity to fermented beverages. Experimenting with different combinations can lead to delightful discoveries and personalized recipes.

Understanding the role of acidity in fermentation is also important. Acidity helps preserve the ferment and creates an environment unfavorable to harmful bacteria. In vegetable fermentation, the natural production of lactic acid by lactic acid bacteria lowers the pH, ensuring safety and longevity. For some ferments, like pickles, adding vinegar can help jumpstart the acidification process, though traditional lacto-fermentation relies solely on salt and the natural microbial activity.

Fermentation hinges on the balance of these tools and ingredients, each playing a pivotal role in the success of the process. Cleanliness and proper sanitation cannot be overstated; always start with clean equipment and sterilized jars to prevent contamination. This attention to detail ensures that only the desired microorganisms thrive, leading to a successful and safe ferment.

For those new to fermentation, starting with simple projects like sauerkraut or yogurt can help build confidence and understanding of the basic principles. As you become more comfortable, experimenting with different ingredients and techniques can open up a world of culinary possibilities. Remember, fermentation is both an art and a science; while precision is important, there is also room for creativity and personal expression.

Incorporating fermented foods into your diet not only enhances flavor and variety but also offers numerous health benefits. The probiotics produced during fermentation support gut health, while the process itself can increase the bioavailability of nutrients. Embracing fermentation can transform your kitchen into a hub of culinary innovation and wellness.

## Techniques Lacto-Fermentation, Alcoholic Fermentation, and Vinegar Making

Lacto-fermentation, alcoholic fermentation, and vinegar making are three distinct yet interconnected techniques that transform raw ingredients into a variety of flavorful and nutritious products. Each method harnesses the power of microorganisms to create unique culinary delights, from tangy pickles and robust wines to aromatic vinegars. Understanding these techniques and their intricacies can open up a world of possibilities for home fermenters and chefs alike.

Lacto-fermentation is one of the oldest and simplest forms of fermentation, relying on lactic acid bacteria to convert sugars in vegetables and fruits into lactic acid. This process not only preserves the food but also enhances its flavor and nutritional value. The key to successful lacto-fermentation lies in creating an environment where these beneficial bacteria can thrive while keeping harmful bacteria at bay.

To start, select fresh, high-quality vegetables. Organic produce is ideal as it is free from pesticides and chemicals that could interfere with the fermentation process. Commonly fermented vegetables include cabbage, cucumbers, carrots, and radishes, but the possibilities are endless. Once you have your vegetables, wash them thoroughly and cut them into desired shapes and sizes. Uniform cuts ensure even fermentation.

Salt is a crucial ingredient in lacto-fermentation. It draws out moisture from the vegetables, creating a brine in which lactic acid bacteria can flourish. The salt concentration typically ranges from 2% to 3% of the vegetable weight. For example, if you have one kilogram of vegetables, you would use 20 to 30 grams of salt. Mix the salt with the vegetables, massaging them to release their juices. Pack the vegetables tightly into a clean fermentation vessel, ensuring they are fully submerged in their own brine or an additional prepared brine solution.

Creating an anaerobic environment is essential. Use fermentation weights to keep the vegetables submerged and prevent exposure to air. Cover the vessel with a lid or cloth to protect it from contaminants while allowing gases to escape. Store the vessel at room temperature, ideally between 65°F and 75°F, and let the fermentation process begin. Depending on the vegetable and desired flavor, fermentation can take anywhere from a few days to several weeks. Taste the ferment periodically to determine when it has reached your preferred level of tanginess.

Alcoholic fermentation, on the other hand, involves the conversion of sugars into alcohol and carbon dioxide by yeast. This process is fundamental in the production of beer, wine, and spirits. The choice of ingredients and the fermentation environment play a significant role in the final product's quality and character.

For wine making, start with high-quality grapes or other fruits. Crush the fruit to release its juices, creating a must. The must is then placed in a fermentation vessel, and yeast is added to kickstart the fermentation process. Wild yeasts present on the fruit's skin can be used, but many vintners prefer commercial yeast strains for their consistency and predictability. The yeast consumes the sugars in the fruit juice, producing alcohol and carbon dioxide. This process can take several days to a few weeks, depending on the temperature and yeast strain used.

Temperature control is critical in alcoholic fermentation. For wine, maintaining a temperature between 60°F and 80°F is ideal. Too high a temperature can kill the yeast or produce undesirable flavors, while too low a temperature can slow down or stall the fermentation. Once the primary fermentation is complete, the wine is often transferred to secondary vessels for aging and clarification. This secondary fermentation can last several months to years, allowing the wine to develop its flavors and complexity.

Beer making follows a similar principle but starts with malted grains, typically barley. The grains are mashed to convert their starches into fermentable sugars, creating a wort. The wort is boiled with hops to add bitterness and aroma, then cooled and transferred to a fermentation vessel. Yeast is added, and the fermentation process begins. Like wine, beer fermentation requires careful temperature control, generally between 65°F and 75°F for ales and 45°F to

55°F for lagers. After primary fermentation, the beer may be conditioned and carbonated before being bottled or kegged.

Vinegar making is a two-step fermentation process that starts with alcoholic fermentation and is followed by acetic acid fermentation. The first step involves creating an alcoholic base, such as wine, cider, or beer. Once you have your alcoholic liquid, it is exposed to acetic acid bacteria, which convert the alcohol into acetic acid, giving vinegar its characteristic sour taste.

To make vinegar, begin with a high-quality alcoholic base. The alcohol content should be between 5% and 10%. Pour the liquid into a wide-mouthed vessel to maximize the surface area exposed to air, which is necessary for the acetic acid bacteria to thrive. Cover the vessel with a cloth to allow airflow while keeping out dust and insects. Store the vessel in a warm, dark place, ideally between 70°F and 80°F.

The acetic acid fermentation can take several weeks to several months, depending on the temperature and the initial alcohol content. Over time, a gelatinous layer known as the "mother of vinegar" may form on the surface. This is a colony of acetic acid bacteria and can be used to start future batches of vinegar. Taste the vinegar periodically to assess its acidity and flavor. Once it has reached the desired level of acidity, strain out any solids and transfer the vinegar to clean bottles for storage.

Each of these fermentation techniques—lacto-fermentation, alcoholic fermentation, and vinegar making—requires careful attention to detail and an understanding of the microorganisms involved. While the processes may seem complex, they are rooted in traditional methods that have been refined over centuries. By experimenting with different ingredients and conditions, you can create a wide range of fermented foods and beverages that are both delicious and nutritious.

Lacto-fermentation offers a way to preserve vegetables while enhancing their nutritional value and flavor. The tangy, probiotic-rich results can be enjoyed on their own or as an accompaniment to various dishes. Alcoholic fermentation transforms simple sugars into complex alcoholic beverages, each with its own unique profile influenced by the choice of ingredients and fermentation conditions. Vinegar making, the final transformation, converts alcohol into a versatile acidic condiment that can be used in cooking, pickling, and preserving.

## Fermented Beverages: Kombucha, Kefir, and More

Kombucha and kefir, two of the most popular fermented beverages, have gained immense popularity for their unique flavors and health benefits. These drinks, rooted in ancient traditions, offer a delightful mix of probiotic goodness and refreshing taste. While they share some similarities, each has distinct characteristics and preparation methods that set them apart from one another. Exploring these beverages, along with other lesser-known fermented drinks, can open up a new world of home fermentation and nutrition.

Kombucha, a slightly effervescent tea-based drink, owes its origins to ancient China, where it was cherished for its supposed health-promoting properties. The process of making kombucha involves fermenting sweetened tea with a symbiotic culture of bacteria and yeast, commonly known as a SCOBY. This gelatinous, pancake-like culture acts as the engine for fermentation, converting sugars into various organic acids, gases, and alcohol.

To start brewing kombucha, you'll need a few basic ingredients: tea (black, green, or a mix of both), sugar, water, and a SCOBY along with some starter liquid from a previous batch or store-bought unflavored kombucha. Begin by boiling water and steeping the tea, allowing it to cool to room temperature before adding sugar. Once the sweetened tea has cooled, transfer it to a clean glass jar and gently place the SCOBY on top, followed by the starter liquid. Cover the jar with a breathable cloth secured with a rubber band to allow airflow while keeping contaminants out.

Fermentation time for kombucha varies but typically ranges from 7 to 14 days, depending on ambient temperature and personal taste preference. Warmer temperatures speed up the fermentation process, while cooler temperatures slow it down. During fermentation, the SCOBY metabolizes the sugar, producing a range of organic acids, vitamins, and minerals, along with a small amount of alcohol and carbonation. Taste the kombucha periodically using a clean straw to determine when it has reached your desired balance of sweetness and acidity.

Once the primary fermentation is complete, you can proceed to a secondary fermentation to add flavor and carbonation. Transfer the kombucha to airtight bottles, adding fruit, herbs, or spices of your choice. Seal the bottles tightly and let them sit at room temperature for a few more days, allowing the natural carbonation to develop. Remember to burp the bottles daily to prevent excessive pressure buildup. After achieving the desired level of fizziness and flavor, refrigerate the bottles to slow down fermentation and enjoy your homemade kombucha.

Kefir, another popular fermented beverage, originates from the Caucasus Mountains and has been consumed for centuries for its health benefits and refreshing taste. Unlike kombucha, kefir is typically made with milk and relies on kefir grains, which are a combination of bacteria and yeast held together by polysaccharides. These grains resemble small, gelatinous cauliflower florets and act as the catalyst for fermentation.

To make milk kefir, start with high-quality milk—cow, goat, or even plant-based milk can work, though dairy milk is traditional. Place the kefir grains in a clean glass jar and add the milk, using a ratio of about one tablespoon of grains per cup of milk. Cover the jar with a breathable cloth or a loose lid to allow gases to escape while keeping contaminants out. Let the mixture sit at room temperature for 12 to 48 hours, depending on the ambient temperature and your taste preference. The longer the fermentation, the tangier the kefir will become.

Once the milk has thickened and developed a slightly tangy flavor, strain out the kefir grains using a plastic or non-metallic strainer, as metal can damage the grains. The strained liquid is your milk kefir, ready to be consumed immediately or stored in the refrigerator. The grains can be reused indefinitely, growing and multiplying with each batch. Rinse them gently with non-chlorinated water if necessary and start a new batch of kefir.

Water kefir is a dairy-free alternative that uses water kefir grains, which are slightly different from milk kefir grains. To make water kefir, dissolve sugar in water and add the water kefir grains. You can also add a slice of lemon, a piece of dried fruit, or a pinch of mineral-rich sea salt to provide additional nutrients for the grains. Cover the jar with a breathable cloth and let it ferment at room temperature for 24 to 48 hours. Once fermentation is complete, strain out the grains and bottle the liquid. Like kombucha, water kefir can undergo a secondary fermentation with added flavors for a fizzy, refreshing drink.

Other fermented beverages worth exploring include tepache, a traditional Mexican drink made from pineapple peels and sweetened with piloncillo or brown sugar. To make tepache, place pineapple peels in a large jar with water, sugar, and spices like cinnamon or cloves. Cover the jar with a cloth and let it ferment at room temperature for a few days until it reaches the desired level of tanginess and effervescence. Strain the liquid and refrigerate it before serving.

Kvass, a traditional Eastern European beverage, is made by fermenting bread, usually rye, with water, sugar, and sometimes fruit. The process involves soaking the bread in water, adding sugar and yeast, and allowing it to ferment for a few days. The resulting drink is slightly alcoholic, tangy, and refreshing. Beet kvass is a variation that uses beets instead of bread, resulting in a vibrant, earthy drink rich in probiotics and nutrients.

Jun is another fermented tea beverage similar to kombucha but made with green tea and honey instead of black tea and sugar. The process of making jun is nearly identical to kombucha, with the primary difference being the ingredients. The jun SCOBY thrives on green tea and honey, producing a lighter and more delicate flavor compared to kombucha.

When diving into the world of fermented beverages, it's essential to maintain cleanliness and monitor the fermentation process closely. Contamination can spoil the batch and pose health risks, so always use clean utensils and containers, and keep an eye on the appearance and smell of your fermenting liquids. Proper storage and handling are equally important to ensure the longevity and safety of your homemade beverages.

Fermented beverages like kombucha, kefir, tepache, kvass, and jun offer a delightful and nutritious alternative to store-bought drinks. They are rich in probiotics, which support gut health and overall well-being. Additionally, the fermentation process can enhance the nutritional profile of the ingredients, making them more bioavailable and easier to digest. By experimenting with different recipes and flavors, you can customize these drinks to suit your taste preferences and dietary needs.

# Recipes Sauerkraut, Kimchi, and Miso

Fermented foods hold a special place in culinary traditions worldwide, often prized for their unique flavors and health benefits. Sauerkraut, kimchi, and miso, three prominent examples, offer a delightful introduction to the art of fermentation. Each of these foods has distinct preparation techniques, flavor profiles, and cultural significance, making them fascinating subjects for home cooks and fermentation enthusiasts alike.

Sauerkraut, a staple in German cuisine, is simply fermented cabbage. Its name translates to "sour cabbage" in German, reflecting its tangy taste. The process of making sauerkraut is straightforward and requires just two essential ingredients: cabbage and salt. Start with fresh, firm heads of cabbage, preferably organic, to ensure the best flavor and texture. Begin by removing the outer leaves, then slicing the cabbage thinly. The thinner the slices, the faster and more uniformly the cabbage will ferment.

Next, place the cabbage in a large bowl and sprinkle it with salt. The salt draws out the cabbage's natural juices, creating the brine necessary for fermentation. The general rule of thumb is to use about 2% salt by weight of the cabbage. Massage the cabbage and salt together vigorously with your hands until the cabbage starts to soften and release liquid. This process, known as maceration, helps to kickstart fermentation by breaking down the cabbage's cell walls.

Once the cabbage has released enough liquid to cover itself when packed down, transfer it to a clean fermentation vessel. Traditional crocks or glass jars work well for this purpose. Pack the cabbage tightly into the container, pressing it down firmly to eliminate air pockets and ensure it is submerged in its brine. If needed, use a weight to keep the cabbage submerged, as exposure to air can lead to spoilage and unwanted mold growth. Cover the container with a cloth or a lid that allows gases to escape.

Fermentation time for sauerkraut can vary, typically taking between one to four weeks, depending on the ambient temperature and your taste preference. Warmer environments speed up fermentation, while cooler ones slow it down. During this period, beneficial bacteria such as Lactobacillus convert the cabbage's natural sugars into lactic acid, which acts as a preservative and gives sauerkraut its characteristic sour flavor. Taste your sauerkraut periodically until it reaches the desired level of tanginess. Once ready, transfer it to the refrigerator to slow down fermentation and preserve its flavor.

Kimchi, a beloved Korean dish, is a spicy and tangy fermented vegetable medley, often featuring napa cabbage and daikon radish. Kimchi's bold flavors come from a combination of fermentation and a variety of seasonings, including chili pepper, garlic, ginger, and fish sauce. To make traditional napa cabbage kimchi, begin by cutting the cabbage into quarters lengthwise and then into bite-sized pieces. Salt the cabbage generously and let it sit for a few hours to draw out excess water, ensuring a crisp final product.

While the cabbage is salting, prepare the kimchi paste by blending together garlic, ginger, Korean chili flakes (gochugaru), fish sauce, and a bit of sugar. This paste is the heart of kimchi, providing its signature heat and depth of flavor. You can customize the paste to your taste, adjusting the amount of chili flakes for spiciness or adding other ingredients like fermented shrimp or anchovy sauce for additional umami.

After the cabbage has wilted and released a significant amount of liquid, rinse it thoroughly to remove excess salt and drain well. Combine the cabbage with the kimchi paste, making sure to coat each piece evenly. Add other vegetables, such as julienned daikon radish, carrots, and green onions, for extra texture and flavor. Transfer the mixture to a clean fermentation vessel, packing it down to remove air pockets and ensure it is submerged in its juices.

Kimchi typically ferments faster than sauerkraut, often being ready to eat within a few days to a week. The fermentation time can vary depending on the temperature and your taste preference. Taste the kimchi periodically, and once it has developed the desired level of tanginess and complexity, move it to the refrigerator to slow down further fermentation. Kimchi can continue to develop its flavor over time, becoming more pungent and sour as it ages.

Miso, a traditional Japanese seasoning, is a fermented paste made primarily from soybeans, salt, and koji—a mold-inoculated grain such as rice or barley. Miso comes in various types, ranging from sweet white miso to robust red miso, each with its own flavor profile and culinary uses. The process of making miso is more complex and time-consuming than sauerkraut or kimchi, but the result is a deeply savory and umami-rich condiment that can enhance a wide range of dishes.

To make miso, start with high-quality soybeans, soaking them overnight to soften. Cook the soaked soybeans until tender, then drain and cool them to room temperature. Meanwhile, prepare the koji by steaming rice or barley and inoculating it with Aspergillus oryzae spores. This mold breaks down the grains' starches into simple sugars, providing food for the fermentation process. The koji needs to incubate in a warm, humid environment for about 48 hours until it is fully colonized by the mold.

Once the soybeans are cooked and the koji is ready, combine them with salt and blend into a smooth paste. The amount of salt used varies depending on the desired type of miso, with lighter misos using less salt and darker misos using more. Pack the mixture into a fermentation vessel, pressing it down firmly to remove air pockets and prevent spoilage. Cover the surface with a layer of salt or a piece of plastic wrap to inhibit mold growth, then seal the container.

Miso ferments slowly, often taking several months to a few years to develop its full flavor. During this time, enzymes produced by the koji break down the soybeans' proteins and carbohydrates, creating a complex array of amino acids, peptides, and sugars. The result is a rich, savory paste with a deep umami flavor that can be used in soups, marinades, dressings, and more. Taste the miso periodically, and once it has reached the desired flavor profile, transfer it to the refrigerator to halt fermentation.

# Chapter 5

# Plating and Presentation

## The Art of Plating

Plating is an art form that transforms a simple meal into a visual masterpiece. It's the final step in the culinary process, where creativity and precision come together to enhance the dining experience. The presentation of food can influence our perception of taste and quality, making it an essential skill for any chef, whether you're cooking at home or in a professional kitchen. Mastering the art of plating involves understanding basic principles, utilizing various techniques, and employing thoughtful design.

The foundation of effective plating starts with balance. Balancing elements on a plate involves considering flavors, textures, and colors. A well-balanced dish not only looks appealing but also ensures that every bite offers a harmonious blend of tastes and sensations. Begin by planning your components: proteins, vegetables, starches, and sauces. Each element should complement the others, avoiding any single overpowering ingredient. For instance, a rich, fatty meat might pair well with something acidic or bitter to cut through the heaviness, such as a citrus salad or bitter greens.

Color plays a significant role in plating. Vibrant, contrasting colors can make a dish more visually stimulating. Think about the natural hues of your ingredients—bright greens, reds, yellows, and purples—and how they can be arranged to create an appealing palette. Avoid monochromatic plates, as they tend to look dull and uninviting. Instead, strive for a variety of colors that will catch the eye and invite curiosity. Fresh herbs, edible flowers, and microgreens can add splashes of color and a touch of elegance to your presentation.

Texture is another crucial aspect. Combining different textures—crunchy, creamy, tender, and crispy—adds interest and depth to a dish. Consider how each element will feel in the mouth and try to offer a range of experiences. A creamy mashed potato can be paired with a crunchy element like fried shallots or roasted nuts. Similarly, a smooth purée can be contrasted with a crisp vegetable or a delicate, flaky pastry. The interplay of textures keeps the diner engaged and enhances the overall enjoyment of the meal.

The choice of plate is your canvas. The size, shape, and color of the plate can either enhance or detract from the presentation. White plates are a popular choice because they provide a neutral background that makes the colors of the food pop. However, don't be afraid to experiment with different styles and colors, as long as they complement the dish. The size of the plate should be appropriate for the portion size; a plate that is too large can make the food look sparse, while a plate that is too small can appear overcrowded.

When arranging food on the plate, think about the rule of thirds, a principle borrowed from photography and art. Imagine dividing the plate into three equal sections both horizontally and vertically, creating a grid. Place the main elements of your dish along these lines or at their intersections. This technique creates a sense of balance and directs the viewer's eye naturally around the plate. Avoid placing everything in the center, as it can look static and uninspired.

Height adds visual interest and dimension. Building up the components of your dish can make it more dynamic. Use ring molds to stack ingredients or layer components to create height. For example, place a bed of risotto in the center of the plate and top it with a piece of seared fish, then add a garnish of microgreens on top. This vertical arrangement draws the eye upward and adds a sense of sophistication.

Sauces and garnishes are the finishing touches that can elevate a dish from good to extraordinary. Sauces should be applied with precision, either by drizzling artfully, creating dots or streaks, or using a squeeze bottle for more intricate designs. Avoid drowning the plate in sauce; instead, aim for a balance that enhances the flavors without overwhelming the dish. Garnishes should be edible and contribute to the overall flavor and texture. Fresh herbs, citrus zest, or a sprinkle of sea salt can add the final flourish.

Negative space, or the empty areas on the plate, is just as important as the food itself. It provides a visual break and helps to highlight the main elements of the dish. Don't feel compelled to fill every inch of the plate. Allowing some space around the food can make the presentation appear more elegant and refined. This minimalist approach emphasizes the quality and importance of each component.

Temperature contrast can also enhance the dining experience. Combining hot and cold elements on the same plate can be intriguing and delightful. A warm piece of meat paired with a chilled salad or a hot soup with a dollop of cold cream can create a pleasing contrast that excites the palate. Ensure that these contrasts are intentional and complementary, enhancing the overall harmony of the dish.

Seasonal and local ingredients not only provide the best flavors but also add a sense of place and time to your plating. Utilizing what is fresh and in season ensures that your dishes are vibrant and packed with flavor. It also allows you to tell a story through your food, connecting the diner to the local environment and the time of year. This practice can lead to more innovative and creative presentations, as you work with the natural beauty of seasonal produce.

Practice makes perfect. The art of plating is a skill that improves with experience and experimentation. Don't be afraid to try new techniques and styles, and always keep learning from other chefs and visual artists. Pay attention to how food is presented in high-end restaurants, cooking shows, and food magazines. Analyze what makes certain plates appealing and think about how you can incorporate those elements into your own presentations.

Incorporating personal touches can make your plating unique and memorable. Whether it's a signature garnish, a particular way of arranging ingredients, or a special plate or bowl, adding elements that reflect your personality or culinary style can set your dishes apart. These details create a connection with the diner, making the meal not just a feast for the stomach, but also a feast for the eyes and the soul.

# Color Theory and Texture Balance

Colors and textures are the unsung heroes of culinary artistry, influencing not just the visual appeal of a dish but also the overall dining experience. Understanding color theory and texture balance can elevate your cooking from ordinary to extraordinary, making every plate a feast for both the eyes and the palate. These elements require a thoughtful approach, blending scientific principles with creative intuition to craft dishes that are as pleasing to look at as they are to eat.

Color theory in cooking begins with the basics of the color wheel. Primary colors—red, blue, and yellow—are the foundational hues from which all other colors are derived. Secondary colors—green, orange, and purple—are created by mixing two primary colors. Understanding this relationship helps in selecting complementary colors that enhance the visual appeal of a dish. Complementary colors, which sit opposite each other on the color wheel, create vibrant contrasts that can make a dish more visually appealing. For instance, pairing the deep green of spinach with the bright orange of roasted carrots can create a striking visual contrast that draws the eye.

Analogous colors, which are next to each other on the color wheel, offer a more harmonious and soothing effect. A dish featuring the yellow of summer squash, the orange of bell peppers, and the red of tomatoes can evoke a sense of warmth and comfort. Monochromatic schemes, using variations of a single color, can be sophisticated and elegant but require careful attention to texture and presentation to avoid looking flat or monotonous.

The psychological impact of color cannot be overstated. Colors can evoke emotions and set the mood for the dining experience. Warm colors like red, orange, and yellow are stimulating and can increase appetite, making them ideal for hearty, comforting dishes. Cool colors like blue, green, and purple are calming and can create a sense of freshness, making them perfect for light, refreshing meals.

Incorporating a variety of colors in a dish is not just about aesthetics; it also often means incorporating a variety of nutrients. Different colors in fruits and vegetables typically indicate different vitamins and minerals. For example, red tomatoes are rich in lycopene, while orange carrots are high in beta-carotene. A colorful plate is not only visually appealing but also nutritionally balanced, offering a range of health benefits.

Texture balance is equally important in creating a memorable dish. Texture refers to the physical feel of food in the mouth, encompassing qualities like crunchiness, creaminess, chewiness, and tenderness. A well-balanced dish offers a variety of textures that keep the diner engaged and satisfied. Imagine biting into a perfectly grilled piece of chicken: the initial crunch of the crispy skin gives way to the juicy, tender meat underneath. This interplay of textures enhances the overall eating experience.

Achieving texture balance involves combining different cooking techniques. Roasting, frying, grilling, and baking can create crispy, crunchy elements, while boiling, steaming, and simmering can produce softer, more tender components. Pairing a crispy element like fried onions with a creamy mashed potato, or a crunchy vegetable like celery with a tender poached fish, can create a delightful contrast that makes each bite exciting.

The use of garnishes can also add textural variety. Toasted nuts, fresh herbs, crispy bacon bits, or a sprinkle of coarse sea salt can provide that extra crunch or burst of flavor that elevates a dish. However, garnishes should be used thoughtfully and purposefully, enhancing the dish without overwhelming it.

Temperature plays a role in texture perception as well. Serving a dish with both hot and cold components can create an interesting contrast. Think of a warm slice of apple pie served with a scoop of cold vanilla ice cream. The juxtaposition of temperatures adds another layer of sensory pleasure to the dining experience.

The size and shape of food also contribute to texture balance. Larger, chunkier pieces can offer a satisfying chew, while finely diced or pureed components can provide a smooth, creamy texture. Varying the sizes and shapes of ingredients on a plate can make each bite unique, preventing monotony and keeping the diner engaged.

Cultural influences often dictate the preferred textures in different cuisines. For example, Japanese cuisine places a high value on delicate, refined textures like the silky smoothness of tofu or the tender chewiness of sashimi. In contrast, many Western dishes celebrate robust, hearty textures, such as the crispiness of fried chicken or the dense chewiness of a freshly baked baguette. Understanding these cultural preferences can inform your approach to texture balance, allowing you to create dishes that resonate with your audience.

Experimentation is key to mastering color theory and texture balance in cooking. Don't be afraid to try new combinations and techniques. Keep a journal of your experiments, noting what works and what doesn't. Over time, you'll develop an intuitive sense for which colors and textures complement each other, allowing you to create dishes that are both visually stunning and delicious.

Presentation techniques can further enhance the impact of color and texture. For example, layering ingredients can create a beautiful visual effect while also combining different textures in each bite. Arranging components in geometric patterns or natural, flowing shapes can guide the diner's eye and make the dish more appealing. Using different plate shapes and sizes can also influence the perception of color and texture, adding another dimension to your presentation.

Incorporating edible flowers and herbs can add pops of color and intriguing textures to your dishes. Flowers like nasturtiums, pansies, and violets are not only visually striking but also offer unique flavors that can enhance the overall taste profile. Fresh herbs like basil, cilantro, and mint can add vibrant color and a burst of freshness that complements many dishes.

Ultimately, the goal of understanding and applying color theory and texture balance is to create a cohesive and enjoyable dining experience. Each element on the plate should work together to create a harmonious whole, where the visual appeal enhances the flavors and textures. As you continue to refine your skills, you'll find that the principles of color and texture become second nature, allowing you to focus on creativity and innovation in your cooking.

## Tools for Artistic Presentation

Mastering the art of culinary presentation begins with understanding the essential tools that can transform a simple dish into a visual masterpiece. Just as a painter relies on brushes and palettes to create a work of art, a chef relies on specific tools to craft visually stunning plates. These tools not only enhance the visual appeal but also ensure precision and consistency in presentation, making each dish a feast for the eyes as well as the palate.

One of the most fundamental tools in artistic presentation is the plating spoon. These specialized spoons, with their long handles and deep bowls, are designed for precise placement and spreading of sauces and purees. Using a plating spoon, you can create delicate drizzles, swirls, and dots that add a sophisticated touch to your dish. A well-executed sauce pattern can frame the main components, drawing the diner's eye to the centerpiece of the plate.

Tweezers are another indispensable tool for chefs focused on meticulous presentation. Culinary tweezers come in various shapes and sizes, allowing for the precise placement of microgreens, edible flowers, and other small garnishes. These fine details can elevate a dish, adding color, texture, and a touch of elegance. With tweezers, you can achieve a level of precision and consistency that would be difficult to attain with your fingers alone.

Molds and rings are essential for creating uniform shapes and layers. These tools come in various sizes and shapes, from simple circles and squares to more intricate designs. By packing ingredients into these molds, you can create visually striking elements that maintain their shape on the plate. For example, using a ring mold to shape rice or vegetables can add a clean, professional look to your presentation, while layering ingredients in a mold can create an impressive terrine or tartare.

Squeeze bottles are versatile tools for adding sauces and purees with precision. These bottles allow you to control the flow of the sauce, making it easy to create intricate patterns, lines, and dots. They are particularly useful for decorating plates with multiple sauces, enabling you to add contrasting colors and flavors with ease. A simple squeeze bottle can transform a plain plate into a canvas for your culinary artistry.

A microplane or zester is a must-have for adding fine, delicate textures to your dishes. This tool is perfect for grating citrus zest, hard cheeses, chocolate, and spices, adding a burst of flavor and a fine, textured finish. A sprinkle of lemon zest or a dusting of Parmesan can brighten up a dish and add a layer of complexity to the presentation. The microplane's ability to create uniform, delicate shavings makes it an invaluable tool for any chef focused on detail.

Piping bags and tips are essential for adding decorative elements and intricate details. These tools are commonly used in pastry work but are equally valuable in savory applications. With a piping bag, you can add dollops of mousse, whipped cream, or purees with precision and flair. Different tips allow for various shapes and textures, from fine lines to elaborate rosettes. Mastering the use of a piping bag can add a professional touch to your presentations, making each plate look meticulously crafted.

A mandoline slicer is a powerful tool for achieving uniform, thin slices of vegetables and fruits. This tool allows you to create delicate, wafer-thin slices that can be used for garnishes, salads, or layered dishes. The consistent thickness ensures even cooking and a polished appearance. Slices of radish, cucumber, or apple can add a crisp, fresh element to your dishes, enhancing both the visual appeal and the texture.

Edible flowers and herbs are natural tools for adding color and elegance to your plates. Choosing the right flowers and herbs can complement the flavors of your dish while adding a vibrant, aesthetic touch. Nasturtiums, pansies, and violas are popular choices for their striking colors and edible qualities. Fresh herbs like basil, cilantro, and dill can add a burst of green and a fragrant finish. Using these natural elements thoughtfully can transform a simple dish into a visually stunning creation.

Brushes are versatile tools for adding fine details and artistic touches. Culinary brushes come in various sizes and can be used for painting sauces, oils, or glazes onto plates and ingredients. A delicate brushstroke of balsamic reduction or a light glaze of herb oil can add a layer of sophistication and depth to your presentation. Brushes also allow for creative techniques like splattering or feathering, adding a unique artistic flair to your dishes.

Heat tools, such as blowtorches, can add dramatic finishing touches to your presentations. A quick pass with a blowtorch can caramelize sugars, melt cheese, or add a charred finish to meats and vegetables. This technique not only enhances the flavor and texture but also adds a visually appealing element. The golden brown finish of a crème brûlée or the charred edges of a roasted pepper can make your dish stand out with a professional touch.

Plates and platters themselves are crucial tools for artistic presentation. The choice of plate can significantly impact the overall look of the dish. White plates are classic and versatile, providing a neutral backdrop that makes the colors of the food pop. Dark or colored plates can add contrast and drama, highlighting specific elements of the dish. The shape and size of the plate also play a role, influencing how the food is arranged and perceived. Square plates can add a modern, geometric feel, while round plates offer a more traditional presentation.

Finally, practice and experimentation are key to mastering the use of these tools. Developing your artistic presentation skills takes time and patience. Start by experimenting with different tools and techniques, keeping a journal of your successes and learning from your mistakes. Over time, you'll develop an intuitive sense of what works and what doesn't, allowing you to create stunning, visually appealing dishes with confidence and creativity.

# Techniques: Smears, Dots, and Streaks

Mastering the techniques of smears, dots, and streaks can dramatically elevate your culinary presentations, transforming your plates into canvases of edible art. These methods, while seemingly simple, require precision and practice to execute flawlessly. When done right, they add depth, contrast, and visual intrigue to your dishes, inviting diners to savor their meals with their eyes before taking the first bite.

Smearing is a foundational technique that can be used to create a base layer or background for other elements on the plate. It often involves using a sauce or puree that has a smooth, pliable consistency. To create a smear, place a dollop of the sauce on the plate and use the back of a spoon, an offset spatula, or even a brush to spread it out in a sweeping motion. The key is to apply even pressure to create a clean, consistent line with a tapered edge. This technique can be used to frame the main components of the dish, add a pop of color, or introduce complementary flavors.

Consider a plate of roasted duck breast. A vibrant cranberry sauce smear can serve as a striking backdrop that not only adds visual appeal but also complements the rich, savory flavors of the duck. The deep red of the cranberry sauce against a white plate creates a dramatic contrast, drawing the eye to the center of the plate where the duck is elegantly arranged. The smooth texture of the smear also adds a creamy element that can enhance the overall mouthfeel of the dish.

Dots, another essential technique, offer a way to add precision and playful details to your presentation. Dots can be created using sauces, purees, or gels that hold their shape well. To create dots, use a squeeze bottle, piping bag, or a small spoon. The size and placement of the dots can vary depending on the desired effect. For a more refined look, opt for small, evenly spaced dots. For a bolder, more whimsical approach, use larger dots in an asymmetrical pattern.

Imagine a delicate plate of seared scallops. Adding small dots of a vibrant pea puree around the perimeter not only introduces a splash of color but also provides bursts of fresh, sweet flavor that complement the buttery scallops. The dots can be arranged in a way that guides the diner's eye around the plate, creating a sense of movement and flow. Additionally, varying the size of the dots can add a dynamic, layered effect that keeps the presentation interesting.

Streaks, similar to smears, are used to create lines and patterns that add energy and direction to the plate. This technique involves dragging a sauce or puree across the plate using a brush, spatula, or even a spoon. Streaks can be straight, curved, or wavy, depending on the desired visual effect. They can be used to connect different elements on the plate, create a sense of motion, or simply add a decorative touch.

Think of a beautifully plated dessert, such as a chocolate tart with raspberry coulis. Creating a streak of raspberry coulis across the plate adds a vibrant, artistic touch that contrasts with the rich, dark chocolate. The streak can be used to anchor the tart, drawing the diner's eye towards the center of the plate. The fluidity of the streak adds a sense of elegance and sophistication, elevating the overall presentation.

Combining these techniques can yield stunning results. For example, a dish featuring grilled salmon can be enhanced with a smear of lemon dill aioli, dots of beet puree, and a streak of balsamic reduction. The smear provides a creamy, tangy base that complements the rich salmon, while the dots add bursts of earthy sweetness. The streak of balsamic reduction not only adds a touch of acidity but also visually ties the elements together, creating a cohesive and harmonious presentation.

To master these techniques, practice is essential. Start by experimenting with different consistencies of sauces and purees to find the ones that work best for each technique. Thicker sauces are generally better for smears and streaks, while slightly thinner sauces work well for dots. Use different tools to achieve various effects and practice applying even pressure to create clean, precise lines and shapes.

Pay attention to the overall composition of the plate. Consider the placement and balance of each element to create a visually appealing and cohesive presentation. Negative space, or the empty space around the elements, is just as important as the elements themselves. It allows the eye to rest and helps to highlight the key components of the dish.

Experiment with color contrasts and harmonies. Bright, vibrant colors can add excitement and energy to the plate, while more subdued tones can create a sense of elegance and sophistication. Use the color wheel as a guide to choose complementary and analogous colors that enhance the visual appeal of your presentation.

Texture also plays a crucial role in these techniques. Smooth, creamy smears can be contrasted with crunchy elements, while the delicate dots and streaks can be paired with more substantial components. This interplay of textures adds depth and interest to the dish, making it more engaging for the diner.

Incorporate these techniques thoughtfully, ensuring they enhance rather than overshadow the main components of the dish. The goal is to create a balanced and harmonious presentation that highlights the flavors, textures, and colors of the ingredients. Avoid overcrowding the plate or adding elements that do not contribute to the overall experience.

As you gain confidence and skill, let your creativity guide you. Each dish presents an opportunity to experiment with new combinations and techniques, pushing the boundaries of culinary presentation. Keep a journal of your successes and learnings, noting what works well and what can be improved. Over time, you'll develop your own style and approach, allowing you to create dishes that are not only delicious but also visually stunning.

## Case Studies Iconic Plated Dishes

The world of cuisine is replete with iconic plated dishes that have stood the test of time, becoming symbols of culinary excellence and innovation. These dishes not only showcase the skills of chefs but also reflect cultural heritage, regional flavors, and historical contexts, making them fascinating subjects for case studies. By examining these iconic dishes, we can uncover the techniques, ingredients, and creativity that contribute to their enduring popularity and influence.

One of the most celebrated iconic dishes is the French classic, **Coq au Vin**. This dish, which translates to "rooster in wine," exemplifies the rustic yet sophisticated nature of French country cooking. Originating from the Burgundy region, Coq au Vin is traditionally prepared with rooster, although chicken is commonly used today. The preparation involves marinating the poultry in red wine, typically a Burgundy, along with onions, garlic, and a bouquet garni of thyme, bay leaf, and parsley. The dish is then slowly braised with bacon, mushrooms, and pearl onions, resulting in a rich, deeply flavored stew. The key to mastering Coq au Vin lies in the slow cooking process, which allows the flavors to meld and the meat to become tender. This dish is a testament to the culinary philosophy of using simple, quality ingredients and time-honored techniques to create something extraordinary.

Moving to Italy, **Risotto alla Milanese** is another iconic dish that has captivated food lovers for centuries. Hailing from Milan, this luxurious rice dish is distinguished by its vibrant yellow color, derived from saffron. The preparation of risotto is an art form, requiring patience and precision. Arborio or Carnaroli rice is sautéed in butter and onions, then slowly cooked with hot broth, added ladle by ladle, while constantly stirring. This technique releases the starches from the rice, creating a creamy texture. The addition of saffron, dissolved in a small amount of broth, imparts a unique flavor and color. The dish is finished with grated Parmigiano-Reggiano cheese and a knob of butter, enriching its creamy consistency. Risotto alla Milanese is often served as a side dish to Osso Buco, another Milanese specialty, showcasing the harmonious pairing of flavors and textures in Italian cuisine.

Japanese cuisine offers another fascinating case study with **Sushi**, an iconic dish that has become a global phenomenon. Sushi, in its many forms, represents the epitome of Japanese culinary precision and artistry. At its core, sushi is vinegared rice paired with various ingredients, most commonly raw fish. The preparation of sushi rice is a meticulous process, involving the washing, soaking, and cooking of short-grain rice, followed by seasoning with a mixture of rice vinegar, sugar, and salt. The fish, often sourced from the freshest and highest quality available, is sliced with precision to ensure the perfect texture and flavor. The balance between the rice and fish, the sharpness of the wasabi, and the umami of the soy sauce come together to create a harmonious bite. Sushi exemplifies the Japanese culinary principles of simplicity, seasonality, and respect for ingredients, making it a revered dish worldwide.

In the realm of American cuisine, **Barbecue Ribs** stand out as an iconic dish that embodies regional diversity and cultural significance. American barbecue, particularly ribs, varies greatly across different regions, each with its own unique style and flavors. For instance, Kansas City-style ribs are known for their sweet and tangy tomato-based sauce, while Memphis-style ribs are typically dry-rubbed with a blend of spices before smoking. The preparation of barbecue ribs involves slow-cooking over indirect heat, often using wood smoke to infuse the meat with a distinct smoky flavor. This low-and-slow cooking method ensures tender, juicy ribs that are rich in flavor. Barbecue ribs are not just a dish but a communal experience, often enjoyed at gatherings and celebrations, reflecting the social and cultural aspects of American food traditions.

From the streets of Bangkok, **Pad Thai** emerges as an iconic dish that has gained international acclaim. This Thai stir-fried noodle dish is a perfect balance of sweet, sour, salty, and spicy flavors. Pad Thai is typically made with rice noodles, stir-fried with a combination of tamarind paste, fish sauce, palm sugar, and chili pepper. It includes ingredients like shrimp, tofu, egg, bean sprouts, and peanuts, each contributing to the dish's complex flavor profile and texture. The preparation requires high heat and quick cooking to prevent the noodles from becoming mushy, ensuring they remain chewy and absorb the sauce's flavors. Pad Thai's appeal lies in its vibrant, harmonious flavors and its ability to be customized with various proteins and vegetables, making it a versatile and beloved dish in Thai cuisine.

In the world of fine dining, **Beef Wellington** stands as a symbol of culinary sophistication and skill. This British dish, named after the Duke of Wellington, consists of a tender beef fillet coated with pâté and duxelles (a finely chopped mixture of mushrooms, shallots, and herbs), then wrapped in puff pastry and baked to perfection. The process of making Beef Wellington requires precision and timing to ensure the beef is cooked to the desired doneness while the pastry remains golden and crisp. The pâté and duxelles add layers of richness and flavor, while the pastry provides a buttery, flaky contrast. Beef Wellington is often served with a rich Madeira or red wine sauce, enhancing its luxurious appeal. This dish exemplifies the artistry and technique of classic European cuisine, making it a centerpiece at celebratory meals and upscale dining establishments.

Exploring the diverse culinary landscape, **Ceviche** from Peru offers a refreshing and vibrant case study. Ceviche is a dish of raw fish marinated in citrus juices, primarily lime or lemon, which "cooks" the fish through a process called denaturation. This dish is typically seasoned with ingredients like cilantro, red onion, chili peppers, and sometimes corn or sweet potatoes, creating a balance of fresh, tangy, and spicy flavors. The key to a perfect ceviche lies in the freshness of the fish and the marination time, which should be just long enough to change the fish's texture without overdoing it. Ceviche is a reflection of Peru's rich marine biodiversity and its culinary tradition of using fresh, local ingredients. It has gained popularity worldwide for its light, refreshing taste and healthful qualities.